STABILITY THROUGH ECONOMIC COOPERATION IN A NUCLEAR ENVIRONMENT

The Regional Centre for Strategic Studies (RCSS) is an independent, non-profit and non-governmental organization for collaborative research, networking and interaction on strategic and international issues pertaining to South Asia. Set up in 1992, the RCSS is based in Colombo, Sri Lanka.

The RCSS is a South Asian forum for studies, training and multi-track dialogue and deliberation on issues of regional interest. All activities of RCSS are designed with a South Asia focus and are usually participated by experts from all South Asian countries. The Centre is envisaged as a forum for advancing the cause of cooperation, security, conflict resolution, confidence building, peace and development in the countries of the South Asian region.

The RCSS serves its South Asian and international constituency by: (a) networking programmes that promote interaction, communication and exchange between institutions and individuals within and outside the region engaged in South Asian strategic studies; (b) organizing regional workshops and seminars and sponsoring and coordinating collaborative research; and (c) disseminating output of the research through publications which include books, monographs and a quarterly newsletter. The RCSS facilitates scholars and other professionals of South Asia to address, mutually and collectively, problems and issues of topical interest for all countries of the region.

Queries may be addressed to:

Regional Centre for Strategic Studies
2 Elibank Road
Colombo 5
SRI LANKA
Tel: (94-11) 2599734, 2599735
Fax: 2599993; e-mail: rcss@sri.lanka.net
RCSS website: http://www.rcss.org

RCSS Policy Studies 31

Stability through Economic Cooperation in a Nuclear Environment

SAIRA YAMIN

REGIONAL CENTRE FOR STRATEGIC STUDIES
COLOMBO

MANOHAR
2005

Published by
Ajay Kumar Jain for
Manohar Publishers & Distributors
4753/23 Ansari Road, Daryaganj
New Delhi 110 002
and
Regional Centre for Strategic Studies
2 Elibank Road
Colombo 5
SRI LANKA
Tel: (94-11) 2599734-5; Fax: 2599993;
e-mail: rcss@sri.lanka.net
Website: http://www.rcss.org

First published 2005

ISBN 81-7304-635-2

Typeset by
Kohli Print
Delhi 110 051

Printed at
Lordson Publishers Pvt. Ltd.
Delhi 110 007

Distributed in South Asia by
FOUNDATION BOOKS
4381/4, Ansari Rorad
Daryaganj, New Delhi 110 002
and its branches at Mumbai, Hyderabad,
Bangalore, Chennai, Kolkata

Contents

RCSS is grateful to the
Nuclear Threat Initiative (NTI) for its
generous support for the RCSS-NTI Award
on which this report is based.

Acknowledgements

This report has been informed by interviews, field research and secondary data. I am immensely grateful and indebted to my colleagues, friends, and family who have helped me in preparing this report. Many of them listened to my ideas and shared theirs very candidly to enhance the contents of my report as well as to maintain objectivity. I have benefited tremendously from the good wishes and support of many of whom unfortunately I will not be able to mention in this space. I owe my profound gratitude also to all those who provided me with the opportunity to interview them on the subject of my research.

I am most grateful to RCSS (Regional Centre for Strategic Studies) and the NTI (Nuclear Threat Initiative) for reposing their confidence in me to conduct this research and providing a very unique opportunity to explore avenues for economic cooperation across the India-Pakistan divide. I am especially thankful to Prof. Sridhar Khatri and Ms. Minna Thaheer for their tireless and kind assistance through every step in the process. The study would not have been possible without them. Many thanks are owed to Dr. Rifaat Hussain for being a wonderful supervisor and painstakingly editing my work. Very special thanks are due to my dear friend Ayesha Siddiqa for providing the inspiration. I must express my heartfelt thanks to Waqar Ahmed from the SAARC Chambers of Commerce and Industry, Islamabad, who helped me get started by virtue of his timely assistance and resourcefulness.

Part of the data collection for this project was conducted in New Delhi. My immense gratitude is owed to Prof. Varun Sahni and Prof. C. Raja Mohan for making it possible for me to visit India at a very short notice and for providing their most insightful advice and suggestions all along the way. Their guidance has helped give direction to the report. The credit for helping identify and interviewing many of the stakeholders in Delhi must be shared with Suba Chandran. If it wasn't for him I may have been lost in the streets of Delhi for months!

I am deeply grateful to my mother Safia for being there for me and for babysitting my four-year old whenever I needed her. Last but not least my friend Rizwana Kamran for her positive attitude and constant reminders that there is light at the end of the tunnel.

SAIRA YAMIN

CHAPTER 1

Background

India and Pakistan, the two nuclear arch rivals in South Asia, are amongst the most impoverished and least developed nations of the world. According to the United Nation's *Human Development Report, 2003*, 34.7 per cent of India's population lives on less than US $1 a day, the share of the poorest 20 per cent in the national income is only 8.1 per cent and 47 per cent of the children are underweight for their age. In Pakistan, the number of people living below the poverty line has gone up from 18 per cent in 1987 to 37 per cent in 2002, 38 per cent of the children are underweight for their age and youth illiteracy stands at 38.4 per cent.[1]

Having gained independence from British colonial rule in 1947, India and Pakistan have not been able to live in peace with each other. Military confrontation has ranged from full-scale wars to border skirmishes and military stand-offs. As a consequence, the economic development of both countries has been undermined. Since their overt nuclearization in 1998, both countries have been earnestly trying to address their differences in order to avert a nuclear confrontation.

POLITICAL BACKDROP

Relations between the two countries in the post-nuclearization scenario have been extremely turbulent and volatile. In 1999, they fought a limited war over Kargil, and in May–June 2002, they came close to fighting a full-scale conventional war.

Despite several instances of conflict escalation, both states have been periodically extending the proverbial olive branch to other.

[1] *Human Development Report*, United Nations Development Programme, 2003.

Within less than a year of the testing of the nuclear devices in May 1998, the then Indian Prime Minister, Atal Behari Vajpayee, took a historic bus ride from Delhi to Lahore in February 1999, to sign the Lahore Agreement with his Pakistani counterpart, Nawaz Sharif. The Lahore declaration which sought to melt the ice between the adversaries came to naught a few months later as Pakistan's army ventured into Kargil along with Kashmiri Muslim militant groups. A limited war between the two nuclear powers ensued to the horror of the global community. President Bill Clinton of the US described South Asia as the most dangerous place on earth and it became evident that unless effectively managed the nuclearization of the India-Pakistan conflict would endanger the security of the entire region.

These mounting international concerns prompted Gen. Pervez Musharraf, the Pakistani military mastermind of the Kargil operation, to extend an olive branch to India. President Musharraf went to Agra in 2001 in a bid to mend fences with India. Although he received an overwhelmingly warm reception from his Indian hosts, he was unable to conclude a peace deal with New Delhi.

The year 2002 witnessed yet another nosedive in Indo-Pakistan relations. Following the mobilization of Indian troops along the western border, Pakistan made reciprocal moves, sparking fears that the two countries were drifting inevitably towards war. While war was narrowly averted thanks to American diplomatic intercession, the economies of both countries suffered on account of the enormous expenditures in maintaining a state of war-readiness.

A year later—towards the end of 2003—Indo-Pakistan relations took a turn for the better with both sides evincing interest in a commitment to resolving their differences through a multi-track approach. A peace process with a focus on a composite dialogue addressing the Kashmir dispute, people-to-people contacts, holding sports and cultural events, and agreements exploring avenues for economic cooperation has begun and is spawning hopes of a rapprochement.

ECONOMIC REALITIES

The economic case for regional trade expansion in South Asia is exceptionally strong, especially when one considers that India is one of the fastest-growing economies in the world. According to World Bank estimates, India's economy would grow up to 8 per cent annually in the next few years. The World Bank reports that in comparison to other industrialized nations, India is likely to achieve impressive growth as the potential is enormous. Pakistan's economy would fare better if it did not have to bear the costs of perpetuating hostility and sustaining the war machine.

Pakistan's GDP stands at a paltry US $295 billion (11 per cent of India's). It spends more than 5 per cent of its GDP on defense. Pakistan's economy is in the phase of recovery. Her debt burden though reduced to 90 per cent of the GDP from 102 per cent of the GDP around four years earlier is still a big burden on the national economy. Foreign Exchange Reserves position is comfortable (US $12.02 billion) but despite these macro-economic indicators Pakistan has attracted very little foreign investment. India on the average attracted around US $4 billion FDI compared to US $45 billion China's average annual FDI in the past few years. Pakistan on average attracted US $500–600 million during the past few years.[2]

India on the other hand can go on increasing its defence allocation without much impact on the rate of economic growth. The normalization of relations with India and a consequent cap, if not reduction, in defence spending could go a long way in helping Pakistan out of its economic woes. A lagging GDP growth rate and mounting fiscal deficit—a direct consequence of the mounting foreign and domestic interest payment liabilities and defence expenditure—have had a damaging impact on the country's finances. There is an urgent need to revive domestic demand, accelerate industrial production and tap foreign markets to boost export earnings. In this context, Pakistan's external economic relations, particularly with India, come into sharp focus.

[2] Saleem Farrukh, 'Time to Strike a Deal is Now', *The News*, Islamabad, 4 January 2004.

Any assessment of the costs of conflict between India and Pakistan should not only take into account the considerable economic and developmental losses but also the low levels of bilateral trade between the two countries. Globalization of the world economy makes it imperative for India and Pakistan to modify their national security policies with a view towards promoting greater regional integration and the pursuit of sustainable development.

All countries of the world are affected by globalization, some positively and others to their disadvantage. To make the most of the benefits of globalization as well as to protect themselves from its adverse effects, many countries have established regional trading blocs. Such Regional Trading Arrangements (RTA) have tremendous potential for economic growth yet, 'South Asia is the only major world region not to move towards regional cooperation and integration.'[3] Therefore, promoting trade relations between India and Pakistan should be seen as a first step towards instituting regional arrangements. As Shahid Javed Burki suggests, 'our policy-makers must be cognizant of the fact that the world is organizing itself into a number of regional arrangements and we in Pakistan cannot afford to be left out of them'.[4]

Sustainable development requires that India and Pakistan build a partnership on the basis of trust and common security concerns such as the pooling of resources, economic cooperation, poverty alleviation, and sharing of best practices.

A paradigm shift in national security policies that calls for regional integration and economic cooperation will draw international investment and development opportunities to South Asia for the benefit of both countries. It is evident that neither Pakistan nor India can make territorial gains in Kashmir through military means. Policy constraints need to be bridged by allowing trade and investment to play a role in evolving a new policy that is based on cooperation instead of confrontation.

[3] Shahid Javed Burki, 'The Themes to be Explored', *Dawn*, Karachi, 23 January 2001.

[4] Ibid.

INTERSTATE TRADE RELATIONS

Bilateral trade between India and Pakistan is abysmally low at less than 1 per cent of their global trade (see Table 1.1). It has been severely restricted by decades of mutual suspicion, conservative and discriminatory policies. Trade within South Asia itself is highly underdeveloped. Moreover, economic linkages and official interaction between stakeholders are negligible, both between India and Pakistan and among the countries that are members of the South Asian Association for Regional Cooperation (SAARC).

In the post-independence period, India was Pakistan's most important and natural trading partner. In the first few years after partition, approximately half of Pakistan's total exports were directed to the Indian market, and a third of its imports came from India. The Indian currency devaluation in 1949, not matched by Pakistan, soon led to a steep decline in trade. Pakistan followed by imposing import restrictions, and from then on trade levels between the. two countries began to decrease.[5]

From 1968-1975, a period that included the war that led to the breakup of Pakistan and the creation of Bangladesh, there was virtually no bilateral trade. In the last three decades, Pakistan and India have devalued their currencies at different times, leading to shifts in their relative price levels. But trade is now so low that these shifts in competitiveness have little overall economic impact. In 2000–01, India's exports equalled US $44 billion, but only US $186 million worth of exports went to Pakistan. India imported US $50 billion worth of goods, but only US $65 million worth of its imports were from Pakistan. For the same time period, Pakistan's total imports were US $10.2 billion and exports equaled US $8.93 billion.[6]

The assessment of the costs of conflict between India and Pakistan surely then needs to take into account the additional expenses incurred by both countries by not tapping the resources available with each other through formalized bilateral trade. It is only common sense that bilateral trade relations would mean

[5] Teresita Schaffer, Mandavi Mehta and Amir Ahmad, 'Regional Economic Relationships: Trade, Energy and Water—Pakistan's Future and US Policy Options', a report from the CSIS project, April 2003.

[6] Ibid.

TABLE 1.1: PAKISTAN'S TOTAL TRADE AND TRADE WITH INDIA 1992–2002

(*in US million dollars*)

	1992–3	1993–4	1994–5	1995–6	1996–7	1997–8	1998–9	1999–2000	2000–1	2001–2
Total Trade										
Export	6,819	6,812	8,141	8,707	8,323	8,627	7,779	8,568	9.201	9,134
Import	9,963	8,561	10,401	11,804	11,894	10,118	9,431	10,309	10.728	10,339
Trade with India										
Export	83	42	42	41	36	89	175	54	55	49
Import	67	70	64	95	197	153	146	127	235	187

Source: State Bank of Pakistan, *Annual Report*, various years, Karachi.

higher employment, increased sources for income generation, reduced transportation costs as well as cheaper goods. In the case of Pakistan, it may even mean cutting health costs by bringing in cheaper medicines from India,[7] while for India it would mean cheaper and adequate energy to support its growing industrialization and consumer requirements.

India and Pakistan are inclined towards trading with states as far away as North America, Europe, the Middle and Far East and much less with each other. Greater trade would translate into increased investments in communications and infrastructure, and an increase in export volume besides other spin-offs including increased revenues from taxes, greater employment and higher incomes. Bilateral trade between India and Pakistan is presently valued at between US $200 and 250 million, while unofficial levels are estimated between one and two billion dollars through third countries such as Dubai, Singapore and elsewhere (see Table 1.2).

E. Sridharan argues that 'India does not import any of Pakistan's major exports. Nor does Pakistan import any of India's major exports.' He explains this fact in terms of trade-related and economic

TABLE 1.2: INDIA–PAKISTAN BILATERAL TRADE

(in US million dollars)

Year	India's Export to Pakistan	India's Imports from Pakistan	Balance of Trade	Total Trade
1997–8	124.97	32.86	92.11	157.83
1998–9	105.52	213.28	(–)107.76	318.80
1999–2000	92.97	68.05	24.92	161.02
2000–1	183.04	62.90	120.14	245.94
2001–2	140.70	63.40	77.30	204.10
2002–3	216.52	46.83	169.69	262.35

Source: Directorate General of Commercial Intelligence and Statistics (DGCI&S), Kolkata.

[7] Jagdish Bhagwati, *A Stream of Windows—Unsettling Reflections on Trade, Immigration, and Democracy*', Cambridge: The MIT Press, 1998, pp. 369–71. Bhagwati argues 'there is clearly tremendous potential to lower medical costs by importing more foreign doctors and exporting more patients'.

(rather than political) arguments, and says that this is because of the competitive rather than complementary nature of the two economies exporting similar products, and argues, that there is the 'general tendency for poor countries to trade with developed ones rather than with their neighbours until a certain level of development has been achieved.' This explains the reasons why trade did not take place between the two countries, and he thinks that 'the real scope for trade and investment is in the future and begins now.'[8]

The present study argues that there is no economic rationale and justification for either of the two countries not to trade with each other, especially in the era of globalization and liberalization and after the setting up of the World Trade Organization, of which both countries are members.

India's principal imports from Pakistan during 1999–2003 included fruits and nuts, sugar, rice, spices, cotton (raw and waste), textile yarn, fabrics, leather, electronic goods, organic chemicals and other crude minerals (see Table 1.3). Pakistan in the same year imported oil meals, drugs, pharmaceuticals, fine chemicals, spices, dyes, rubber products, paints/enamels/varnishes, plastic and linoleum products, ores and minerals, primary and semi-finished iron and steel, inorganic/organic agrochemicals from India (see Table 1.4).

India's major export destinations are the United States, Germany, Japan, United Kingdom, Belgium-Luxembourg, United Arab Emirates, Hong Kong, Saudi Arabia, Singapore, Italy, France, South Korea, Malaysia, Australia, China, Netherlands, Indonesia, Bahrain, Philippines. Its major import rsources are the United States, Germany, Japan, the United Kingdom, Belgium-Luxembourg, United Arab Emirates, Hong Kong, Saudi Arabia, Singapore, Italy, France, South Korea, Malaysia, Australia, China, Netherlands, Indonesia, Bahrain, Switzerland, Nigeria, Iran.

Pakistan's major export destinations are the United States, Japan, Germany, the United Kingdom, United Arab Emirates, Saudi Arabia, Hong Kong, Italy, South Korea, Netherlands,

[8] E. Sridharan, 'Economic Cooperation and Security Spillovers: The case of India and Pakistan', in Michael Krepon and Chris Gagne, eds., *Economic Confidence Building and Regional Security*, The Henry L. Stimson Center, Report no. 36, Washington, October 2000.

TABLE 1.3: INDIA'S PRINCIPAL IMPORTS FROM PAKISTAN

Sr. No.	Item	2000–3	2001–2	2000–1
1.	Fruits & Nuts (excluding Cashew Nuts	8.41	26.08	25.43
2.	Plastic & Linoleum products	25.59	21.65	13.76
3.	Drugs, Pharmaceuticals & Fine Chemicals	20.65	17.93	18.03
4.	Rubber manufactured products except Footwear	13.53	7.90	7.87
5.	Dyes/Intermediates & Coal Tar Chemicals	19.46	7.20	8.15
6.	Inorganic/Organic/Agro-chemicals	16.56	6.61	20.18
7.	Iron Ore	17.19	4.67	3.65
8.	Oil Meals	5.66	4.31	17.93
9.	Other commodities	25.36	4.00	4.67
10.	Spices	3.61	3.16	7.56
11.	Tea	4.34	2.95	6.68

Source: DGCI&S, Kolkata.

TABLE 1.4: INDIA'S PRINCIPAL EXPORTS TO PAKISTAN

Sr. No.	Item	2000–3	2001–2	2000–1
1.	Sugar	6.38	41.85	55.60
2.	Plastic & Linoleum products	25.59	21.65	13.76
3.	Drugs, Pharmaceuticals & Fine Chemicals	20.65	17.93	18.03
4.	Rubber manufactured Products except Footwear	13.53	7.90	7.87
5.	Dyes/Intermediates & Coal Tar Chemicals	19.46	7.20	8.15
6.	Inorganic/Organic/Agro-chemicals	16.56	6.61	20.18
7.	Iron Ore	17.19	4.67	3.65
8.	Oil Meals	5.66	4.31	17.93
9.	Other commodities	25.36	4.00	4.67
10.	Spices	3.61	3.16	7.56
11.	Tea	4.34	2.95	6.68

Source: DGCI&S, Kolkata.

Belgium-Luxembourg, and its major import sources are the United States, Japan, Germany, United Kingdom, United Arab Emirates, Saudi Arabia, Kuwait, China, Malaysia, Italy, South Korea, Switzerland, Netherlands, France, Australia, Iran, India.[9]

SAARC AND SAFTA

Indo-Pakistan bilateral ties have witnessed an unprecedented thaw since the holding of the SAARC Summit in January 2004 in Islamabad. Amongst the achievements of the summit was the signing of a South Asia Free Trade Agreement (SAFTA) by the seven-nation forum. SAFTA holds a great promise for the South Asian region which is one of the world's most populous yet least developed, despite possessing tremendous potential for economic growth. With the launch of the free trade zone in the year 2006, it is expected that bilateral trade between India and Pakistan could easily hit anywhere between two and five billion dollars, possibly more. Making SAFTA workable would create an environment that would attract foreign investment. A large number of multinationals are already stepping into the Indian market, and with the opening of intraregional trade more are likely to venture in.

While trade restrictions between India and Pakistan have impeded economic cooperation in the past, subsequent to the signing of the SAFTA the prospects for India Pakistan trade relations appear bright. For instance, historic trade fair titled 'Made in Pakistan' was organized in New Delhi, in March 2004.[10] The aim of the fair was to promote trade between India and Pakistan as well as allay concerns that a South Asian Free Trade zone would lead to Indian goods flooding Pakistani markets. The India-Pakistan balance of trade currently favours the former but Pakistani products have great market potential in India.

The exhibition which was the first of its kind in India had close to three hundred exhibitors participating from across the border. The nine-day fair showcased Pakistani handicrafts, spices,

[9] SAARC reports.

[10] www.saarcchamber.com, 3 March 2004.

fizzy drinks, fashion garments, onyx, melamine products, surgical instruments, hi-tech electronics, glassware, pharmaceuticals, bicycles, and other consumer goods.

By opening up trade with India, Pakistan can export many of these products and more with an advantage. It can also cut costs by importing items such as tea, pharmaceuticals, textile machinery, transport equipment, and iron ore from India, which are otherwise imported from countries as far away as Kenya, Germany, Australia, and Brazil. Consumers also stand to benefit from such an arrangement. There is a complementarity of interests which needs to be capitalized for the countries' mutual advantage. Consider Pakistan and India's major export and import inventories.[11] Pakistan's principal exports are cotton yarn, garments and hosiery, cotton cloth, raw cotton, rice, synthetic textiles, leather, sports goods, carpets and rugs, fish and fish products, surgical instruments, footwear, chemicals, and pharmaceuticals. Its principal imports are non-electrical machinery, petroleum and products, transport equipment, iron and steel products, edible oils, electrical goods, chemicals, fertilizers, grain, pulses, flour, medicines, non-ferrous metals, tea, paper board and stationery, dyes and colour, and silk yarn.

India's principal exports are gems and jewellery, textiles and garments, chemicals and pharmaceuticals, leather, machinery and instruments, marine products, metal products, carpets, oil meals, rice, transport equipment, electronic goods, primary and semi-finished iron and steel, dyes and intermediates, plastic and linoleum products, iron ore, tea, coffee, spices, cashew, petroleum products, rubber, fresh and processed fruits and vegetables, tobacco, non-ferrous metals and software. Its principal imports are crude petroleum and petroleum products, machinery, pearls and precious or semi-precious stones, gold and silver, electronic goods, organic and inorganic chemicals (coal and coke), iron and steel, non-ferrous metals, transport equipment, manufactured fertilizers, edible oils, machine tools, medicinal and pharmaceu-

[11] Information on imports and exports has been drawn from the 'Economic Surveys of India and Pakistan', 2003–4 and SAARC reports.

tical products, pulp and waste paper, newsprint, paperboard and manufactures, pulses, crude fertilizers and minerals.

There is a long list of items that show the commonality of economies and trading patterns of the two countries. There are sectors such as power and information technology in which both India and Pakistan could link up. While India is a global IT superpower, Pakistan has a competitive edge in power generation, areas in which both countries could benefit from each other substantially. Pakistan could very well serve as the transit route for an energy pipeline from Iran and Central Asian States, which would save India the revenue it would otherwise be spending on more expensive means of acquiring power.

Agriculture is pivotal for both countries for achieving higher economic growth rates. Its contribution towards the GDP of both countries is around 25 per cent.[12] This sector offers the largest share of employment in both states and contributes substantially towards the textile sector. Pakistan's textile is the main source of foreign exchange, i.e. around 66 per cent. Pakistan's low-value textile sector such as grey cloth, yarn, thread and spinning is more developed than the value-added textile sector (garments, knitwear, hosiery, apparel) of India. The variation in products can be mutually beneficial. Pakistan has been trying during the fiscal year 2003–4 to modernize its value-added textile sector. Other areas where Pakistan has an edge over India are dairy products, fisheries, fruits and vegetables.

Sectors such as tourism also need to be opened up for collaboration. Sports and sociocultural exchange are activities that are positively projected by the media and would serve to build bridges across the divide.

[12] 'Economic Surveys of India and Pakistan', 2003–4.

CHAPTER 2

Research Objectives

This study aims at analysing the potential of bilateral trade and other economic activities between India and Pakistan, and its impact on improving peace and stability in the region. The focus is on understanding how cooperation in a non-military field might contribute towards improving relations to a degree that could have spin-offs for overall relations in a nuclear environment. The study looks at the current level of formal and informal trade between the two countries and also considers other areas that could be explored for enhancing bilateral economic cooperation.

The Problem

Traditionally, security has been perceived in the traditional framework as meaning military security. However, one knows that there is a holistic approach to security as well that links social and economic security with the broader issue of national security. If one was to tie this concept to the issue of conflict resolution in the India-Pakistan case, one could comfortably argue that increased economic cooperation is something that would not only be beneficial for the respective economic development of both states but would also lead to greater peace building between the traditional rivals, India and Pakistan. Greater peace and stability in turn would result in a major dividend in terms of regional stability and greater economic development.

Thus far, scanty work has been done on the issue of economic cooperation. In fact, the problem is that the absence of research in this area has not allowed policy makers, academics, or other concerned parties to look at the issue of how even traditional rivals could develop stakes in each others' security if there was economic cooperation. One of the basic hypotheses of this research project is that once both sides begin to see the benefits accruing from economic cooperation, it would result in the building of greater bilateral stakes in each others' economic and overall security and stability.

Until now there have been random arguments on the subject on both sides of the divide, but there is an absence of a solid body of research to substantiate any point in favour or against the aforementioned argument. While the picture is clear on the dividends that economic cooperation would produce for India, in Pakistan, there is far less information available and discussions being conducted on the subject.

The primary goal of this study is to evaluate the prospects of an enhancement of economic cooperation between India and Pakistan and its impact on peace and stability in the region. Here, it must be mentioned that there are other such cases from which lessons could be drawn. For instance, the role played by economic activities such as trade and investment in managing the hostile Sino-Indian relations. It is a moot point if Beijing and New Delhi could have managed their political conflict better or worse if they did not have economic stakes in each other's countries.

To assess the earlier hypothesis, the present author has tried to establish a greater and clearer sense of the following:

- The current level of formal economic activities between the two countries
- Informal economic activities between the two countries that could be converted into formal
- The existing official mechanisms and processes that hamper the conversion of informal into formal activities or block the growth of formal bilateral economic activities
- The potential of bilateral economic activities including areas that could be unilaterally or mutually beneficial
- The attitudes of the stakeholders including the political leadership, bureaucracies, and business or other communities towards enhancing economic cooperation

METHODOLOGY

The research has been based on both primary and secondary information. The secondary information pertains to official data on formal and informal trade between India and Pakistan or economic cooperation in key sectors of the economy such as agriculture or others. This data has been helpful in assessing not only the current trends but also in evaluating the problems. Furthermore the study also looks at the available official documents that shed some light on the official position on the subject.

This information has been used along with some primary data in the form of interviews (see Appendix 1, pp. 82–3) to argue the pro-posed case. The interviews include views of officials from trade and commerce, the business community, economists, academia and journalists. Opinions regarding the impact of possible growth and economic cooperation on peace and stability have also been documented. Conversely, the impact of the lack of economic cooperation on the lack of peace and stability in the region has been examined. The two sets of information/data have been evaluated to arrive at a conclusion on the issue of economic cooperation.

REVIEW OF LITERATURE

The literature on economic cooperation between India and Pakistan referred to in this report shows that there are three components to trade: formal import and export of merchandise, which is very low; circular or informal trade through 'third' countries; and the illegal, or suppressed, trade transacted unofficially across the borders. Official trade is hindered by tariff barriers and non-tariff barriers. It is therefore so little that neither country makes it to the top ten trading partners of the other. However, the volume of informal trade between the two countries demonstrates the tremendous potential of bilateral trade between them. Indian tyres, the textile machinery, tea, coffee, chemicals, and drugs are in demand in Pakistan; however, the consumers have to pay highly for these goods since they come through indirect routes. Consumer consciousness is also very low, therefore, awareness needs to be enhanced.

On the surface, trade opportunities appear to be limited given the volatile political relations between the two countries. Pakistan discourages strong economic ties with India for two reasons—one, the fear of Indian goods swamping the Pakistani market; and two, the fear of the Kashmir issue being sidelined in favour of increased economic cooperation. However, both these fears are not based on substantial grounds. Pakistan has free trade with China and yet is not facing much difficulty in competing with Chinese goods. India has a vast market of its surplus goods in Pakistan. The Indian trader is also averse to looking in this direction due to unstable relations and the erratic political climate.

However, by opening up trade with Pakistan, India will stand to benefit immensely through the land route access to Central Asian markets through Pakistan. Normalized economic relations would generate economic gains for both countries. Indian manufacturers could exploit the existing markets in Pakistan whereas Pakistani consumers would pay substantially lower prices than they do at present, for Indian goods. Pakistani manufacturers could easily tap India's large market size. India provides an overwhelmingly huge market of 1.5 billion people to the Pakistani entrepreneur, which needs to be thoroughly explored.

Joint ventures, especially in infrastructure and information technology projects, between India and Pakistan would be attractive proposals for foreign investors. Such initiatives will, therefore, pave the way for attracting foreign direct investment and generate higher revenues for the two impoverished and underdeveloped countries.

The literature on the scope for economic cooperation between the two countries also reveals that the real potential between India and Pakistan lies in the energy sector. Both countries have a huge requirement for natural gas and should seek the economically viable option of importing gas from Central Asia and Iran through joint pipelines. At the same time, there is potential in jointly harnessing and distributing hydropower. Granting transit rights will also open up huge markets for India in Central Asia, and for

Pakistan in the South Asian countries. Clearly the benefits of economic liberalization for both countries are quite obvious and need to be given due consideration by the powers that be.

Economic ties would inevitably promote people-to-people contact, bring about regional integration, create stakes in continuing cooperation and enhance mutual confidence between the antagonists. Eventually both countries would feel compelled to resolve the main issue of conflict so that they are able to co-exist in a peaceful environment conducive to stronger economic ties. Thus, the primacy of economics in India-Pakistan relations can serve as a catalyst in the resolution of the political conflict between the two countries.

If armed conflict could be avoided, India and Pakistan could achieve much higher growth rates with sound economic management. However, these growth rates are not high enough to have a positive impact on alleviating poverty or to bring the two countries at par with the key economic players of the world.

If India and Pakistan want to leap forward into the realm of developed countries by 2020 or 2025, they would require much higher growth rates, in the order of 10 per cent for India and 7 per cent for Pakistan.[1] But such high growth calls for both countries to mobilize their resources in the right direction.

Both India and Pakistan need to fill the investment gap by attracting huge FDIs, unlocking the rural economy, and tapping the black economy. The former will require a stable political and economic environment, transparency and speedy decision-making. The latter will require social reforms. Major political reforms are also the need of the hour.

Needless to say both countries should have peaceful relations with all their neighbours in the South Asian region in order for trade to flourish. Thus, only a long, durable and sustainable peace between them can allow India and Pakistan to concentrate completely on internal political and economic reforms and to achieve the required economic growth rates.

[1] *Cost of Conflict Between India and Pakistan*, Strategic Foresight Group of the International Centre for Peace Initiative, Mumbai, 2004.

At present, joint ventures and direct investment between the two countries are non-existent. Indian and Pakistani products continue to compete in the global market; however, there are many areas of enterprise in which both the countries can complement each other and produce cost-effective quality goods without compromising their interests. Potential areas for cooperation include agricultural products, tyres, auto spare parts, minerals, chemicals, pharmaceuticals, leather, textile, and telecommunications.

Exchange of technology and skills between the two will also help enhance the quality of their goods at comparatively lower costs. Telecommunication networking between them will promote closer interaction between the people at all levels.

Free intra-country tourism would ensure people-to-people contact, which, with the passage of time, will soften mutually intransigent attitudes. Hostilities will eventually fade away and an environment conducive to political, economic, and social cooperation will be built. Joint tourism, especially, in the Himalayan region, could provide a fillip to the tourism industry in both countries.

India and Pakistan can launch joint ventures to harness and transmit the region's hydropower resources. Collaboration in water management and hydropower projects would have a multiplier effect on the benefits of irrigation, minimizing the risks of floods, and establishing an India-Pakistan electric grid system for intra-country transmission of electricity.

India and Pakistan require large volumes of natural gas imports to meet their current and future demands. They can collaboratively tap the major gas deposits of the Persian Gulf and Central Asia. Of the various solutions available, the import of natural gas through a pipeline is the most cost-effective way. A single, joint natural gas pipeline extending overland from Pakistan to India would be economically more feasible for both countries than opting for independent pipelines.

It is estimated that Pakistan can earn approximately US $600–800 million per pipeline per year in transit rights; an additional incentive for Pakistan to act as a supply route for India.[2] At the

[2] *Status Paper: India Pakistan Economic Relations*, FICCI, New Delhi, 2003.

same time, importing gas through a joint pipeline can serve as a cheaper option for India than imports of LNG. However, India fears that Pakistan will use the pipeline as a strategic weapon in the eventuality of a conflict. The level of mistrust between the two countries is extremely high and the core unresolved issues need to be addressed in order for both countries to tread the path of economic cooperation.

Interlinked power and gas networks will generate interdependence between India and Pakistan, which may compel the nuclear arch rivals to resolve their differences.

CHAPTER 3

The Benefits of an Open Economy

Economists generally recognize two broad classes of benefits, the first being static and the second dynamic. Adam Smith and David Ricardo have taught us that trade helps an economy by allowing it to specialize in what it does best. Adam Smith argued that the division of labour—or specialization—enhances productivity, but noted that the degree to which an individual or a nation could specialize depended entirely on the extent of its market. A state which does not open its economy to the international market would also have to produce and manufacture everything in isolation. Its capacity to do so would be restricted to its resources and capabilities. On the other hand, if a group of states could trade amongst themselves, each could specialize in the production of what it is best at, thus producing more than would be possible were their attentions divided among goods that they are less skilled at making. Then they each could trade with their neighbours for the goods that they in turn are good at producing. This would improve the efficiency and economy of scales.

It might even be the case that one country is better than everyone else at producing every commodity. Such an argument is often invoked in order to prove that a developed country cannot benefit from trade with an otherwise underdeveloped country. But it turns out that the argument in favour of free trade prevails over this debate. All that is required is for a country to be relatively less skilled than another in the production of some goods in order for it to benefit from trade. This thesis is in line with the doctrine of 'comparative advantage'—the fundamental principle that underlies the theory of international trade.

The above discussion summarizes the 'classical' view of the benefits of free trade. It is important to note that the benefits from trade under the classical doctrine are primarily static in nature, i.e. they affect the level of output. As explained by Janet Jellen, 'moving from a situation in which there is less trade (or no trade) to one in which trade is freer raises output, but this is more along the lines of a one-time increase (even though it might take a number of years for the benefits from trade to be fully felt). This is not to dismiss the significance of these static benefits: for example, some economic historians have argued that most of the economic growth that occurred in the classical world was rooted in the expansion of markets that took place as a result of increased sea trade around the Mediterranean.'[1]

It appears that the theory of functionalism and neo-functionalism (propounded by economists David Mitrany[2] and Ernst B. Haas[3]), which provided the conceptual framework for the process of regional integration the world over, has very little appeal in the subcontinent. South Asia's experiment with regionalism—through the South Asian Free Trade Area (SAFTA)—has remained a non-starter because two of its important member-countries cannot trade on account of 'insurmountable historical problems'.

The International Relations (IR) theory and the trade theory on regional economic integration approach the issue of economic integration quite independently of their respective world views. The IR theory is more concerned with the security aspects underlying trade ties between states. It offers the liberal and conversely the realist views to economic interdependence suggesting that trade is a precursor either to war or to peace.

The liberals 'tend to argue that economic interdependence lowers the likelihood of war by increasing the value of trading over the alternative of aggression: interdependent states would rather trade than invade. As long as high levels of interdependence can be maintained, liberals assert, we have reason for

[1] Much of this discussion on Smith and Ricardo has been drawn from 'The Continuing Importance of Trade Liberalization', by Janet L. Jellen in *Business Economics*, January 1998.

[2] David Mitrany, *The Functional Theory of Politics*, New York, London School of Economics & Political Science, St. Martins Press, 1975.

[3] Ernst B. Haas, *Beyond the Nation State: Functionalism and International Organisation*, Stanford: Stanford University Press, 1964.

optimism.'[4] On the other hand the realists argue that 'high interdependence increases rather than decreases the probability of war.... Accordingly, interdependence—meaning mutual dependence and thus vulnerability—gives states an incentive to initiate war, if only to ensure continued access to materials and goods.'[5]

The liberal stance is that trade is more profitable and constructive than war, especially for interdependent states. They posit that high trade levels would promote socio-economic development leading to greater internal stability. The liberal perspective contends that with interdependence the environment would become conducive for ongoing cooperative relationships. Economic cooperation and peopl-to-people contact would, therefore, become a forerunner to peace. At the same time political ties between trading partners would strengthen on account of increased trade.[6]

The realist position, on the contrary, states that interdependence in trade and economic relations can induce war since crucial imported goods can be embargoed during a crisis. Therefore, the level of interdependence and the cost of cutting the cord would help determine whether the economic and trading relations could be broken, whether by war or even simply by a suspension of economic and trade relations. In such a scenario, explains the realist view, the potential costs for severed trade, as well as the future prospects of trade, would help decide whether to trade or not to trade. The potentially large costs of having to adjust if trade is discontinued would also play a critical role in any decision to change the trade regime. 'If there are few benefits from trade and few costs if trade is cut off then trade does not matter much in the state's decision to go to war. When dependence is high, peace will be promoted only when the state has positive expectations of future trade.'[7]

[4] Dale C. Copeland, 'Economic Interdependence and War: A Theory of Trade Expectations', *International Security*, vol. 20, no. 4, 1996, pp. 5–6.

[5] Ibid., p. 6.

[6] Ibid., p. 8.

[7] Ibid., p. 25.

Various IR theorists postulate that while absolute gains from trade do to some extent explain the choice between war and trade, relative gains, where the balance of trade favours one more than the other, may also affect decisions to trade or not, especially if the relationship between the states is otherwise not harmonious. Even where there are absolute gains for both countries, 'in general, states will fear the relative gains of nearby, powerful, offensively armed, and hostile nations more than those of distant, weak, defensively armed, and friendly ones.'[8] Another contention is that 'a state must always first consider the division of gains from cooperation in order to guarantee that its partner does not profit more and thus become able to threaten it.'[9] Such considerations regarding future losses and gains affect decisions having a bearing on whether or not to trade.[10]

In sharp contrast to the IR theory which focuses on security concerns, the trade theory addresses the economics of the issue—benefits of trade, regional economic integration, preferential trading agreements, customs unions, inter alia.

Trade theory is primarily concerned with the benefits and gains to be had from economic interdependence, and efficiency and welfare gains, for producers, consumers and governments in case of a trade regime. The theory advocates free trade, with reduced or zero tariff barriers as well as eradication of non-tariff barriers. Empirical research demonstrates that free trade has the potential to reap immense benefits for a nation.

Furthermore, the economics of international integration suggest that countries that form 'regional trading blocs, gain in efficiency and welfare terms, and there are gains; there is increased specialization and increased production, economies of scale are introduced which expand the market size resulting in further gains due to longer production runs and therefore lower costs, and there is increased competition which has positive effi-

[8] Peter Lieberman, 'Trading with the Enemy: Security and Relative Gains', *International Security*, vol. 21, no. 1, 1996, p. 151.

[9] John C. Matthews, III, 'Current Gains and Future Outcomes: When Cumulative Relative Gains Matter', *International Security*, vol. 21, no. 1, 1996, p. 112.

[10] R.J. Barry Jones et al., *Introduction to International Relations*, Manchester: Manchester University Press, 2001.

ciency and welfare consequences; even trade between similar and therefore competitive, as opposed to complementary, products between countries increases as intra-industry trade takes place implying the growth of specialization within industries; larger markets are also said to attract increased foreign direct investment. A result of all this is supposed to be reflected in, amongst other things, improved national income for partner countries.[11]

THE RATIONALE FOR REGIONAL ECONOMIC INTEGRATION

The post-World War II era has seen the emergence of a number of regional trading blocs in Asia, Africa, Europe and America. Data show that nearly 60 per cent of world trade is now conducted on a preferential basis.[12] The creation of economic blocs in various parts of the world has facilitated international trade and protected those blocs from fluctuations in world economy. The experience of these economic blocs shows that the social and economic development of any country will benefit by linking up to the global economy as part of a regional bloc rather than independently.

An integrated regional economy boosts the economic development of a country through the advantages of geographic proximity (such as lower transportation costs and time constraints), and economies of scale in production and infrastructure. Member countries of regional economic blocs are also better able to interact in the global systems of finance, investment, trade, and institutions. The countries that are not part of a trade bloc face the risk of discrimination of their exports and loss of competitiveness, and may be vulnerable to adverse fluctuations in the

[11] Akbar S. Zaidi, 'Pakistan's Development Options: Does India Matter at All?', Paper presented at the Deterrence Theory and South Asia workshop, as part of the University of Pennsylvania Institute for the Advanced Study of India project 'International Relations Theory and South Asia: Towards Long-range Research on Conflict Resolution and Cooperation-building', New Delhi, 26–27 August 2003.

[12] S.K. Mohanty, 'Regional Trade Liberalization Under SAPTA and India's Trade Linkages with South Asia: An Empirical Assessment', RIS Discussion Paper, New Delhi, May 2003.

global economy.[13] The global environment provides a historically unprecedented scale of private capital flows, trade opportunities, information and technology, which, if utilized, can dramatically transform the material conditions of life of the countries of South Asia.

Western Europe was the first region to adopt regional economic cooperation in 1949, with the formation of the European Coal and Steel Community and the foundation of the European Economic Community (EEC) following the 1957 Treaty of Rome.[14] The EEC gave a fillip to the trends in regional integrations and subsequently a number of sub-regional and regional cooperation schemes came up in different parts of the world.

The late 1980s and early 1990s saw a strong trend towards regional economic integration particularly among the developed countries. A European Single Market was evolved by 1992. The USA, Canada, and Mexico formed a Regional Trade and Investment Agreement (RTIA) called NAFTA. A new customs union known as MERCOSUR came up in South America (including Argentina, Brazil, Paraguay, and Uruguay). The Andes countries (Bolivia, Colombia, Ecuador, Peru and Venezuela) formed a Free Trade Area, and the ASEAN Free Trade Area comprising Indonesia, Malaysia, Philippines, Singapore and Thailand also materialized.[15]

Thus, in the light of global trends, irrespective of the pros and cons of the academic debate, South Asia has been pushed to adopt regional economic integration. Economic cooperation, however, has been very limited even though SAARC (South Asian Association for Regional Cooperation) has been in place since 1985. Simultaneously, most South Asian economies were also engaged in accelerating the liberalization of their economies unilaterally. Thus, the impetus for regional economic cooperation came not

[13] Akmal Hussain, 'Peace, Poverty and Economic Growth in South Asia: A Policy Framwork', paper presented at Institute of Regional Studies Conference in Islamabad, June 2004.

[14] Ashfaque H. Khan, and Mahmood Zafar, 'Trade and Regional Economic Cooperation', in *Pakistan Journal of Applied Economics*, vol. 14, nos. 1 and 2, 1998.

[15] Ibid.

only from events shaping the global economy, but also from within the region.

There have also been subregional cooperation agreements in Asia such as BIMSTEC (comprising Bangladesh, India, Myanmar, Sri Lanka and Thailand). However it was not until the late 1980s that South Asian governments made an explicit commitment towards promoting an economic agenda. A Committee for Economic Cooperation (CEC) set up in 1991, to examine a proposal for a South Asian Preferential Trade Agreement (SAPTA), was accepted by all seven member states of the South Asia Association for Regional Cooperation (SAARC) in 1993, and SAPTA came into formal operation in December 1995 with the ratification of the first round of tariff concessions.[16]

The question of increased economic cooperation takes centre stage because of the vital importance of regional cooperation for sustainable economic development of the region. South Asia in general and India and Pakistan in particular have suffered because of political instability and a hostile relationship. India under Congress rule was inclined towards a state-controlled economy which did not want to open itself up to the international market. The socialist policies of the Congress gave India at best a 4 per cent growth rate till it opted to liberalize its economy in the early 1990s.[17]

Pakistan, on the other hand, made enviable economic progress in the 1960s, despite internal turmoil and political instability. However, it could not maintain the same momentum of growth during the next two decades. The decade of the 1990s proved to be the worst in terms of economic development.[18]

Regional economic stagnation persisted for a minimum of ten years after SAARC came into being. The specific reasons for it were that none of the SAARC member states then opted for bold economic reforms. India held on to the policy of protecting

[16] Mohanty, 'Regional Trade Liberalization Under SAPTA, op. cit.

[17] M. Sharif, 'SAFTA: Will it Turn Around the Regional Economies?', in *The News*, 19 January 2004, Islamabad.

[18] Ibid.

her market and the Indo-Pak political conflict held the entire South Asian region back from developing meaningful trade relations.

The consequences of living with political conflicts, adopting protectionist and non-integrative economic policies holding against the wind of globalization, and remaining indifferent towards growing regional economic models severely limited the prospects of economic gains for SAARC countries, benefits that would have otherwise accrued because of the enhancement of regional trade, increased foreign investment, human resource development, and innovation to improve industrial and agricultural sectors. Some of the economic indicators give credence to this stark reality. The SAARC region's share in global trade is around 1 per cent intra-regional trade is around 4–5 per cent of member states' exports and SAARC's total GDP is 1.5 per cent of the global GDP.[19]

'Intra-region per capita income varies steeply between US $600 (for Sri Lanka the highest) and US $180 (for Bhutan, the lowest). In direct contrast to the low SAARC intra-regional trade, the world's leading integrated regions, the EU and the ASEAN, have 60 per cent and 25 per cent intra-regional trade, respectively. The most important question is: will SAFTA provide an opportunity to enhance intra-regional trade to any reasonable percentage? The answer to this question should be positive but it is difficult to quantify at this stage.'[20]

In addition to poor economic indicators in the SAARC region, the region suffers because of illiteracy, gender biases, high maternal and infant mortality, poverty, governance, religious extremism, and other socio-economic ills, which indirectly affect economic growth and regional cooperation.

The opportunity to enhance trade ties through the SAFTA framework gives India and Pakistan a lot of leeway to move forward despite restrictive policy constraints. At the same time the two states need to work on mechanisms that would allow them to

[19] Ibid.

[20] Ibid.

have bilateral trade relations. While economic interdependence may undermine the sovereignty of nations, the question arises whether the Indian economy is able to manage without dependence on Pakistan and vice versa?[21] The benefits and profits of such interdependence would be so high that both parties would avoid situations which would compel them to fight. The potential for economic cooperation between the two sides is tremendous.

[21] Interview with Bharat Karnad, Centre for Policy Research, New Delhi, 19 July 2004.

CHAPTER 4

Lessons from Sino-India Cooperation—A Case Study

In the aftermath of the 2004 SAARC summit there is hope that the Indo-Pakistan peace process will stay on course and proceed in the spirit of the January 6 Islamabad Declaration. The peace process between India and Pakistan has the potential to succeed if complemented by strong trade ties.

Scepticism still abounds, though. There have been many false starts in the past and the two sides remain tentative. But there are sound reasons for hope, too. Both sides have their reasons to seek peace—India to realize its full potential; Pakistan to get out of the dire straits in which the policy of conflict has landed it. It could work. But there is another argument for cooperation, and it can be empirically proved.

Many states with troubled pasts have successfully buried the hatchet. Countries that have tied their economic systems with bilateral and regional trade agreements tend not to use military means to settle political differences. Then there are states that continue to have irritants but avoid a zero-sum competition. Sino-US and Sino-Indian relations are a good study of multilayered relations. Taiwan remains a burning issue between Beijing and Washington, but that does not preclude the two sides from trading and cooperating in other areas (North Korea, for instance). Similarly, India has sought to put the border dispute with China on the back-burner to exploit through cooperation the possibilities a more normal relationship promises. Japan has close relations with the US despite the nuclear bombings of Hiroshima

*This chapter has been drawn from Saira Yamin, 'Lessons of Sino-India Cooperation', in the *Daily Times*, Lahore, 22 March 2004.

and Nagasaki by the latter; the same is true of the growing US-Vietnamese relations. The list is long.

There is a subtext for India-Pakistan relations in the growing Sino-Indian relations. But first some background is in order.

Relations between India and China began to sour when the latter occupied Tibet in 1951. China's annexation of Tibet made the location of this frontier a matter of direct dispute between the two. India claimed a strip of the Tibetan territory as its own. Since then, Sino-Indian relations have remained tense because of boundary disputes, allegations of force projection at the border, and disruptive covert activities by secret agencies. India also claimed China was illegally occupying 38,000 sq km of Indian territory in Kashmir, besides 5,180 sq km ceded by Pakistan to China. Beijing, for its part, laid claim to 90,000 sq km of territory in Arunachal Pradesh, and refused to recognize Sikkim as an Indian state. The 'Sikkim issue' was one of the irritants that hindered Indo-China bilateral ties from moving ahead. Earlier, China had strongly objected to the Himalayan state's 1975 accession to the Indian Union.

India and China have seen well over half a century of hostility and one short war in 1962. But things began to change with the then Indian Prime Minister Rajiv Gandhi's 1988 visit to China. Both governments agreed to set up a Joint Working Group to develop conditions for a 'fair and reasonable settlement' and 'maintain peace and tranquility in the border region.' Subsequently, Chinese Premier, Li Peng visited India in 1991. The two sides signed a number of agreements on diplomatic exchanges, border trade, and science and technology. In 1993, Narasimha Rao, India's Prime Minister at the time, signed the Peace and Tranquility Agreement in Beijing. The visits laid the ground for military CBMs between the two sides in 1993 and 1996, and the formulation of Mutual Understanding, Mutual Accommodation and Mutual Adjustment for a long-term Sino-Indian boundary solution.

Relations nosedived after India's May 1998 nuclear tests and statements from New Delhi pointing to China as the number one threat to India. But deft diplomacy since then has managed to control the damage and put relations back on track. Prime

Minister Vajpayee's visit to China in June 2003, was a major success and the two states are now making headway towards settling their differences.

The normalization process has been fruitful despite China's close diplomatic and military ties with Pakistan. The process entails exchanges in the economic, cultural and technological arenas, and greater people-to-people contact. Relations seem to be moving towards cooperation rather than conflict.

While Sino-Indian trade is still a small percentage of China's trade with other states like the US (which hit a historic high of US $126 billion in 2003), and South Korea (US $44 billion—having increased tenfold in the past decade), the economic and trade cooperation between the two sides has developed very quickly. Bilateral trade has increased from US $5 billion in 2002 to US$ 7.5 billion in 2003 even as the Sino-Pak trade volume has risen to a meager US $2.4 billion in comparison. It is estimated that trade between China and India could surge to US $10 billion by 2005. An ambitious forecast by an Indian diplomat claims that within a decade bilateral trade would hit the US $20 billion mark.

India's exports to China grew by 85.3 per cent during the first nine months of 2003, totalling US $2.95 billion, compared with US $1.59 billion during the corresponding period in 2002. China's exports to India increased by 28.4 per cent during the period as China shipped goods worth US $2.37 billion, compared with US $1.84 billion during the first nine months of 2002. India reported a favourable trade balance of US $584 million during the first three quarters of 2003, compared with a deficit of US $452 million during the same period the previous year.

The rising volume of trade between India and China has compelled both countries to settle their political differences amicably. The two sides are aware that the resolution of the boundary dispute will help them fully normalize their relations. China's Foreign Ministry has quietly stopped showing Sikkim as a separate country. This is a tacit acceptance by Beijing of New Delhi's position. For its part, India has evinced its support to China on the issue of Tibetan autonomy, declaring that it was a territory of the People's Republic of China. It appears to be a quid pro quo.

The maturing of Sino-Indian relations provides ample evidence that increased economic cooperation is not only beneficial for the economic development of states but it also leads to a greater desire for peace by creating vested interests on both sides of the divide. However, as Prof. V.P. Dutt, the former pro-Vice-Chancellor of University of Delhi says, despite improvement in bilateral relations, the mistrust between India and China still exists. 'Both countries, in spite of their social problems, should have closer coordination and cooperation. For peace, there should be greater social cohesion.'[1]

The lesson for South Asia is clear: the road to peace will not be without hiccups, but increased interaction and economic activity can help normalize relations.

SAARC AND INDIA-PAKISTAN TRADE RELATIONS

India and Pakistan have a long and chequered history of bilateral trade relations. Soon after independence, India was Pakistan's biggest and most important trading partner. In 1948–9, Pakistan's exports to India were 56 per cent of its total exports (mostly from the former East Pakistan) and its imports were 32 per cent of the total imports.[2] But Pakistan's quest for industrialization and the non-resolution of political conflicts, gradually made trading between the two countries prohibitive.

Eighty per cent of SAARC's intra-regional trade is to and from India (see Figs 4.1–4.3). An important factor is the large size of the Indian market and its geographic location within SAARC. India has a stronger, finer and broader industrial base. Some of its products like steel, autos, electronic goods, garments, medicines, and software are of comparatively better quality and more cost effective[3] (see Table 4.1). Pakistan's industrialists have entertained

[1] Tara Chand Memorial Lecture organized by India-China Friendship Association at Panjab University, Chandigarh, 15 March 2004.

[2] Sharif, 'SAFTA: Will it Turn Around the Regional Economies?', op. cit.

[3] Ibid.

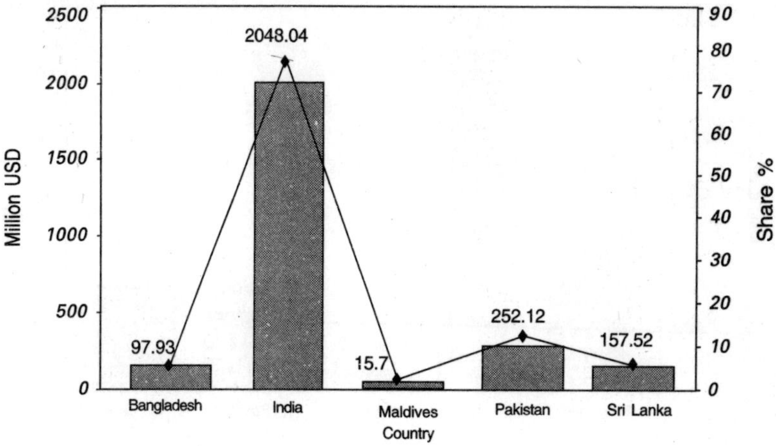

Source: Ananya Raihan, *SAFTA: LDC Perspective*, Centre for Policy Dialogue, Dhaka, Bangladesh.

FIG. 4.1: SHARE OF SAARC COUNTRIES IN INTRA-REGIONAL TRADE: EXPORT 2001

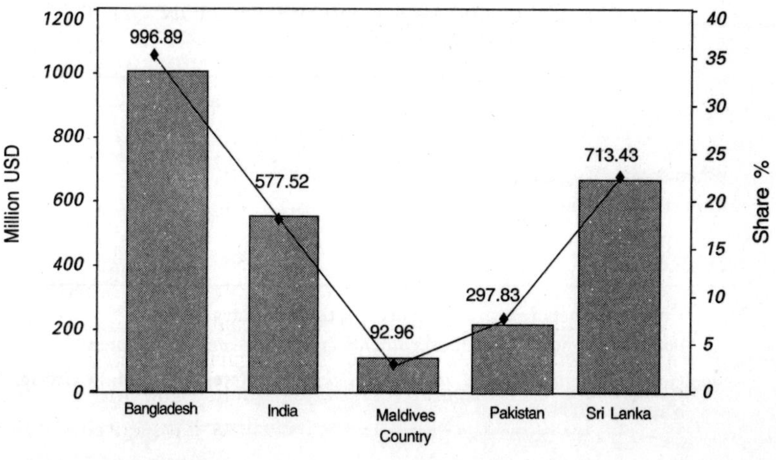

Source: Ananya Raihan, *SAFTA: LDC Perspective*, Centre for Policy Dialogue, Dhaka, Bangladesh.

FIG. 4.2: SHARE OF SAARC COUNTRIES IN INTRA-REGIONAL TRADE: IMPORT 2001

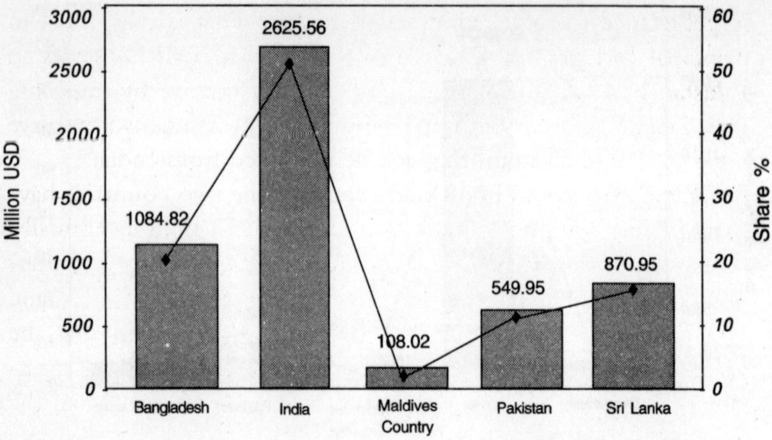

Source: Ananya Raihan, *SAFTA: LDC Perspective*, Centre for Policy Dialogue, Dhaka, Bangladesh.

FIG. 4.3: SHARE OF SAARC COUNTRIES IN INTRA-REGIONAL TRADE 2001

TABLE 4.1: PAKISTAN'S COST REDUCTION ON IMPORTS FROM INDIA

Sector	Percentage per unit
Steel	50
Finished engineering goods	10
Transport equipment	25
Bicycles	20
Pharmaceuticals	30

Note: Current Beneficiaries: Smugglers and third country agents, Potential Beneficiaries: Governments and legitimate businessmen.

Source: *Cost of Conflict between India and Pakistan*, Strategic Foresight Group, Mumbai, 2004.

fears in the past that open trade with reduced tariff rates would be a big advantage to India, swamping the Pakistani markets.

India remains interested in boosting trade relations with Pakistan and has demonstrated its commitment to this effect despite its reluctance to settle political differences. 'That is why India in principal [*sic*] granted "Most Favored Nation" (MFN) status to Pakistan in 1995. But it made trading less attractive by imposing high tariff. Pakistan did not reciprocate but maintains a positive list of 600 trading items that can be imported from India.'[4]

Official barriers to boost trade between the two countries have kept trading volume low to around US $237 million annually. Interviews with stakeholders reveal that illegal trade involves smuggling of items such as betel nut, Rayban glasses, sugar, videos and CD, finished textile goods, etc.[5] Empirical data reveals that the volume of trade is estimated to be around US $1.5 billion annually. Informal trade through third countries such as Dubai, the UAE, and Singapore, involving items like pharmaceuticals, cosmetics, chemicals and viscose has been taking place for the past several years. M. Sharif writes that, 'there is a widespread belief among the trading communities of the two countries that with the introduction of SAFTA rules, trading between the [*sic*] India and Pakistan would get a boost and may touch the US $4 billion mark within a few years.'[6] (see Fig. 4.4)

ECONOMIC REALITIES AND SCOPE

With a view to enhancing Indo-Pak economic relations an awareness of some of the economic realities of the two countries will give a better picture of the scope of trading the two countries can engage in. India is an emerging giant with a huge market, high economic growth rate of more than 8 per cent, and exports of around US $100 billion.[7] It produces internationally competitive products of steel, software, medicine, autos, textiles, etc. There is strong awareness among the Indian political and business leaders that their economic policies have severely constrained India from

[4] Ibid.

[5] For information generated through interviews in New Delhi and Islamabad, see Appendix 1.

[6] Sharif, 'SAFTA: Will it Turn Around the Regional Economies?', op. cit.

[7] Government of India, *Economic Survey, 2003–4.*

Current Official Trade
(average annual figures per year during the period from 2000–1 to 2002–3):
$200–250 million

↓

Third Country Trade:
$1 billion

↓

Contraband Trade:
$1–2 billion

↓

Loss of Government Revenue due to loss of Customs Duties (at 20 per cent)
$0.20–0.40 billion

↓

Potential Trade in Conducive Environment:
$3–4 billion

↓

Trade under SAFTA
(expected): $5 billion

Source: *India Pakistan Economic Relations: A Report*, FICCI, New Delhi, March 2004.

FIG. 4: LOSS OF BILATERAL TRADE

opening up to the world economy, putting it at a visible economic disadvantage.

India attracted little foreign direct investment in the past and therefore in the past five or six years, India has tried to make up for this lag by increasing bilateral trade with China. The volume of trade between them stands at US $10 billion annually, and is growing rapidly. Presently, the balance of trade between the two states lies in favour of India, its primary export to China being iron ore. 'India-ASEAN trade accounts for around US $12.5 billion at present. India is ambitiously working to increase its volume by 250 per cent in the next 5 years.

'Also to its credit India maintains a 1 to 4 ratio in her imports-exports to SAARC countries. It has [an] overall US $2 billion trade surplus with them at present. Its trade surplus with Pakistan is around US $175 million.'[8]

TO TRADE OR NOT TO TRADE

Economics has assumed a pivotal role in the foreign policy exercise among states since the end of the Second World War. History is witness to the fact that even countries of war-ravaged Europe demonstrated their wisdom by deciding to set aside their mutual political and security issues in the interests of enhancing bilateral and multilateral economic interactions and social development. This led to the establishment of the European Union, which stands as a precursor to the military and economic security of the continent.

The issue of fostering greater economic and trade interactions with India has been a controversial political issue in Pakistan. For nearly two decades after independence, India was a major trading partner for Pakistan. But since the 1960s, there has been a steady decline in India's official share in Pakistan's total trade and is now less than 1 per cent. This happened despite the increase in the list of freely importable items from 42 in 1975 to 601 in 1998. The Government of Pakistan links any movement on trade and economic cooperation with Kashmir. This stance often leads

[8] Sharif, op. cit.

one to ask whether political differences between countries should inhibit trade. On the other hand, can economics overlook politics?

When tensions mount the environment does not remain conducive for long term sustainable economic relationships. Despite India's eagerness to develop trade relations with Pakistan more as a matter of the logic of economics then to resolve political differences, its trade policy is moving sluggishly to open its markets to foreign commerce. India has also taken the initiative in suspending rail, road, and air links with Pakistan during political crisis situations. Trade is clearly hindered by a high level of mistrust and complete lack of confidence on both sides.

As a confidence-building measure India may consider removing all ballistic missiles from its western borders unilaterally.[9] Pakistan in the past has taken unilateral measures to build confidence such as the ceasefire in Siachen.[10]

The current Indo-Pakistan peace process is highly vulnerable to the vicissitudes of domestic politics in each country. The harsh reality is that the ruling elites in both countries have yet to recognize the imperatives of placing greater premium on 'economics' than on 'domestic political compulsions'. In the event of a political impasse or a military stalemate, any social, cultural and economic interaction could come to a screeching halt. The governments may suspend all communication links, deny visas, prevent exchanges, and propagate an unfavourable image of the other as they have been prone to do in the past. The importance of political and military confidence building measures, along with enhancement of trade relations, therefore, must not be overlooked.

Building trust requires both countries to remove the irritants in the way of harmonious social, political, and economic exchanges. It appears that for a while the political leadership on both sides of the divide has been sending out dovish signals without meaningfully addressing the conflict of interests. Putting

[9] Interview with Bharat Karnad, Centre for Policy Research, New Delhi, 19 July 2004.

[10] Interview with Mariana Babar, Islamabad, 29 August 2004.

political issues on the back-burner would discourage traders from moving forward as the environment remains unstable and potentially explosive.

The peace rhetoric is an essential element of the formula and the emerging thaw in relations is needed to create room for give and take. Nonetheless symbolism must be supplemented by a sincere and comprehensive process of conflict resolution which needs to address all the issues for both parties.

The signing of SAFTA offers more than a ray of hope. But it must be supplemented by India-Pakistan bilateral agreements. Both the Indian and the Pakistani governments must agree not to disrupt communication links. At the same time, treaties signed must be respected and honoured.

As guided by the IR theory so long as India and Pakistan maintain hostile relations there will be an aversion to trade by the weaker for fear of providing advantage to its adversary. As long as Kashmir remains unresolved it would not be in Pakistan's interests to participate in mutual sustainable development initiatives. Economic interdependence would also undermine its sovereignty. Pakistan does not want to be dependent on trade with India arguably because of the fear that India may cut its supply lines in case of a crisis.

Kashmir is also an emotional issue for the people of both countries. To what extent can Indian and Pakistani policy makers compromise on their respective intransigent positions is anyone's guess. It is India and not Pakistan that has been reluctant to address the issue. There needs to be give and take on Kashmir by both sides, and the aspirations of the people of Kashmir must be given highest priority, come what may. It is worth mentioning that it is in India's economic interest to resolve Kashmir. Kashmir being a nuclear flashpoint is an inhibiting factor for foreign investors. If the dispute is resolved, it would bring about stability in the region and the political climate would be improved. The threat of a nuclear war would be greatly reduced and India would be able to attract more foreign direct investment. Furthermore, the road to wider economic cooperation in the region would be clear.

A SHORT HISTORY OF THE INDO-PAK CONFLICT

British India was partitioned into India and Pakistan as part of the independence process on 14–15 August 1947. The Majority of the Muslim areas in the west (now all of Pakistan) and the east (the place now called Bangladesh) formed Pakistan. The British allowed the nominal rulers of several hundred 'princely states,' to choose between India and Pakistan. However, the Hindu ruler of Kashmir, which had a vast majority of Muslims, remained indecisive.

In the year following partition, Kashmir was divided into a Pakistani-controlled part and an Indian-controlled part consequent to an Indo-Pak military confrontation. This de facto partition continues to this date with the dividing line being known as the Line of Control (LOC).

In 1948, India took the Kashmir issue to the UN Security Council, which passed a resolution calling on Pakistan to do all it could to 'secure the withdrawal' of Pakistani citizens and 'tribesmen' and asking that a plebiscite be held to determine the wishes of the people of Kashmir. However, the UN resolutions were not able to effect either a force withdrawal or a plebiscite.

In 1965, war between India and Pakistan exptected along the India-West Pakistan border and the Line of Control in Kashmir. The UN managed to broker a ceasefire and withdrawal to pre-war lines affirmed by the leaders of the two countries at a 1966 summit meeting in Tashkent, in the former USSR.

In 1971, Bengal, the eastern wing of Pakistan, fought a war of independence with Indian military support and Bangladesh came into being.

Subsequent to the partition of Pakistan, India and Pakistan signed a peace accord in 1972, known as the Simla Agreement, according to which both sides agreed 'to settle their differences by peaceful means through bilateral negotiations or by any other peaceful means mutually agreed upon between them.' Both countries agreed that they would not unilaterally try to alter the Line of Control in Kashmir.

In 1974, India tested a nuclear device and Pakistan, in turn, accelerated its nuclear weapons programme. In the late 1980s and early 1990s, Hindu fundamentalism began to become more powerful as a political force in India and militancy rose in Kashmir. With the intensification of violence by Islamic militants in Kashmir, Pakistan allegedly began to support cross-border infiltration. The Indian military responded with repression to the terrorism, foreign infiltration, and the domestic insurgency. Serious human rights violations continue to this day.

In 1998, India and subsequently Pakistan carried out nuclear weapons' tests and declared themselves nuclear weapon states. The following year.

A terrorist attack on India's Parliament 13 December 2001 left the entire Indian nation in a state of panic. Fourteen people (including five attackers, as well as security guards and two civilians) were killed. Indian decision-makers held the Pakistani government responsible for the attacks and moved hundreds of thousands of soldiers to the border with Pakistan, including the Line of Control in Kashmir. Pakistan reacted by amassing its troops to confront the enemy. The military stand-off continued for a while and finally the crisis was diffused with the help of US intervention.

INDIA'S TRADE TIES WITH OTHER STATES IN SOUTH ASIA

Interviews with stakeholders in New Delhi reveal that where India's security is not threatened, as in its trade relationship with Sri Lanka, it is willing to provide asymmetrical advantage to smaller countries.[11] This tendency, therefore, makes it more feasible and attractive for much weaker countries to trade with the South Asian giant as compared to Pakistan whose military balance is more or less at par with India's (see Tables 4.2 and 4.3).

India has a Free Trade Agreement (FTA) with Sri Lanka. For many years India had been importing rubber from Sri Lanka for the manufacture of tyres. After the FTA, many Indian tyre com-

[11] Interview with Nagesh Kumar, RIS, New Delhi, 22 July 2004.

TABLE 4.2: SAFTA: EXPORT

Partner/Country Reporting Country	Bangladesh	Bhutan	India	Maldives	Nepal	Pakistan	Sri Lanka	Total (SAARC)	World	Share (%) of SAARC Countries in World Exports
Bangladesh	–	1.36	59.74	0.01	0.94	32.55	3.33	97.93	5,681.76	1.72
Bhutan	na	–	na	na	na	na	na	na	na	na
India	1,013.13	7.68	–	27.14	216.76	145.58	637.76	2,048.04	44,306.50	
Maldives	0.00	0.00	0.28	–	0.00	0.00	14.78	15.07	76.58	19.67
Nepal	na	na	na	na	–	na	na	na	na	na
Pakistan	118.68	0.23	54.52	1.77	2.29	–	74.62	252.12	9,246.49	2.73
Sri Lanka	10.06	0.00	71.95	50.32	0.33	24.86	–	157.52	4,672.00	3.37
Total								2,570.68	63,983.33	4.02

Note: NAFT: 62%, EU 45%, ASEA 25%.

Source: Ananya Raihan, *SAFTA: LDC Perspective*, Centre for Policy Dialogue, Dhaka, Bangladesh.

TABLE 4.3: SAFTA: TRADE BALANCE

Partner/Country Reporting Country	Bangladesh	Bhutan	India	Maldives	Nepal	Pakistan	Sri Lanka	Total (SAARC)
Bangladesh	–	na	–821.753	0.01	na	–79.613	–7.408	–908.773
Butan**	na	–	na	na	na	na	na	na
India	821.753	na	–	40.548	na	175.318	534.262	1,571.881
Maldives	–0.001	na	–40.548	–	na	–1.204	–15.387	–57.14
Nepal**	na	na	na	na	–	na	na	na
Pakistan	79.613	na	–175.318	1.204	n.a	–	43.427	–51.074
Sri Lanka	7.408	na	–534.262	15.387	na	–43.427	–	–554.894

Source: Ananya Raihan, *SAFTA: LDC Perspective*, Centre for Policy Dialogue, Dhaka, Bangladesh.

panies shifted to the island nation and started to export from there. Both countries stand to make enormous economic gains. Sri Lanka also offers itself as a free-trade access route to India for foreign companies. Thus far, two sets of bilateral tariff reductions have been agreed on, between India and Sri Lanka and between India and Bangladesh. The Indo-Sri Lanka agreement has become a great success despite some teething pains. It was signed in December 1998 by the two national leaders against strong resistance from their respective Commerce Ministries. India was given three years to bring down tariffs to zero, while Sri Lanka has been given eight years. The agreement has notably granted Sri Lanka greater access to Indian markets, which has given the former considerable benefits despite the fact that Sri Lanka's main exports of tea and garments are barred from India. In the five years following the agreement, the trade gap between the two nations has narrowed by two-thirds, from fifteen to one to five to one. India's exports to Sri Lanka grew from US $430 million in 1997–8 to US $520 million.[12]

USA'S ROLE IN NORMALIZING RELATIONS BETWEEN INDIA AND PAKISTAN

The US has played a very positive role in pushing both countries towards normalizing relations with each other. However, the role of superpowers remains effective only in preventing and diffusing crisis situations between India and Pakistan and in effect superpowers have not been able to resolve protracted conflicts in the region. Whenever there is a power asymmetry, as in the case of India and Pakistan, it is difficult to achieve a win-win outcome without external intervention. It would, therefore, be crucial for the US to maintain its proactive role in moving conflict resolution mechanisms forward.

[12] Schaffer et al., 'Regional Economic Relationships', op. cit.

CHAPTER 5

The Commercial Dimensions

India and Pakistan are South Asia's two largest economies. Trade relations between India and Pakistan have hovered around US $ 200–250 million in the last several years. This is substantially low as compared to India's trade relations with other neighbours like Sri Lanka, Nepal, and Bangladesh. The experience of successful trade relations between the US, Canada and Mexico, shows that the larger economy does not necessarily swamp the smaller neighbouring economies. Sino-India trade relations where the balance of trade favours the latter is another case in point.

Historically, India and Pakistan have been a common market but political issues have prevailed over the logic of trade. Pakistan's economic margin of safety is also much narrower as its foreign exchange reserves are much smaller, therefore, it needs to find alternative means to bolster it.

Although much is made of the rather limited volume of trade between India and Pakistan, a number of points, especially from the Pakistani angle, have been overlooked. First, the quantum of official trade between the two countries, of between two and three hundred million dollars, needs to be supplemented by illicit trade, and the trade of goods which originates in either country but is imported through a third country.

This recalculation increases the total trade between the countries by a factor of four or five. This is a significant increase, especially when one considers the fact that already, for Pakistan at least, using the official bilateral trade figures alone, India is the main trading partner in the SAARC region.

Travel restrictions are the biggest constraint to interstate trade and commerce. The opportunity costs that both Pakistan and India are losing, are tremendous. Both governments are losing valuable revenue to smugglers and third countries.

The complementarities in the structure of the two economies, opportunities for joint ventures with reduced infrastructural costs, price advantages, low freight costs on account of contiguous land borders, and cultural and linguistic similarities provide the rationale for enhanced trade and commerce between the two sides. The logic of economies should therefore be allowed to prevail.

A Ministry of Commerce study of the Government of Pakistan argues that there are numerous advantages to trade between neighbours, as there are low transportation costs, cultural similarities which influence taste and cause profitable complementariness to emerge. In addition, transaction costs are also lowered and such trade 'facilitates the flow of ideas and knowledge that strengthen international competitiveness'. The study looks at a number of sectors in the Pakistan economy and concludes that *'the economic benefits of liberalizing trade with India outweigh costs'*. Consumers in Pakistan will benefit 'unambiguously' because of lower prices, and the government will get far greater revenue from legalizing the existing illicit border trade. Moreover, 'important segments of producers would also benefit because of increased competitiveness and market access to a much larger Indian economy'.[1]

The agriculture sector, which constitutes the most important component of GDP and is the single largest source of employment in both countries, provides numerous avenues for extensive cooperation. Increased business in food and agro-products has a very positive ripple effect on other sectors of the economy. Similarly, Pakistan has distinct advantages in electric power, cotton, and textile production, while India can make a positive contribution in engineering industries and the supply of household goods.

Since the 1970s India has accorded the Most Favoured Nation (MFN) status to Pakistan, whereas Pakistan's trade policy is discriminatory towards India in this respect. India on the other hand has imposed high-tariff and Non-Tariff Barriers (NTB) on its

[1] Government of Pakistan, Ministry of Commerce, *Pakistan-India Trade: Transition to the GATT Regime*, Islamabad, September 1996.

imports which prohibit Pakistan from increasing its exports to India. High-tariff nations, such as India, would lose substantial government revenues from any tariff reductions.

Unofficial trade between India and her neighbours (particularly Bangladesh and Pakistan) could, however, be converted to official trade, resulting in significant revenues for the governments concerned. In 1999–2000. Sri Lanka's exports to India increased from US $27 million to 46 million. In 2002, Sri Lanka exported US $167.7 million worth of goods to India, an increase of more than 135 per cent on the US $70.8 million in 2001. This makes India the destination for 3.5 per cent of Sri Lanka's exports of US $4.8 billion, a sharp rise from the earlier pattern. This suggests that persistence in implementing agreements and expanding tariff reduction can expand the smaller neighbours' share of the large Indian market.[2]

According to World Bank estimates, free trade between the two countries has the potential to multiply ninefold over a period of five to ten years.[3] Trade between India and Pakistan is severely restricted. It is very important for the economic partnership between India and Pakistan to grow. As far as the distribution of international investment patterns is concerned, some of the most important determinants are geographical and cultural proximity. They are natural trading partners such as Brazil and Argentina; Malaysia, Thailand and Singapore; and China and North Korea. Proximity and ethnic similarities are reasons such partnerships thrive.[4]

Although political and religious tensions have curbed such a partnership between the nuclear archrivals in the past, small steps have to be taken where both sides perceive immediate gains.

[2] Schaffer et al., 'Regional Economic Relationships', op. cit.

[3] Estimates of the potential effect of liberalizing trade depends on how one estimates this 'grey area' trade and what assumptions one makes about reductions in tariff and non-tariff barriers. One 1993 study prepared for the World Bank estimates that free trade would result in a ninefold increase in official trade, whereas simply removing the import bans now in place while extending MFN and maintaining a 50 per cent tariff rate would increase trade by a factor of three.

[4] Interview with Nagesh Kumar.

There should be arrangements for buy-back transactions. Both must be see trade as a win-win situation.

Hypothetically speaking, if India desires to export automobiles to Pakistan, in return, the latter must be able to immediately sell some product to India. A framework for simultaneous transactions must be evolved. However, the transactional balance so far has not been addressed. The government and industrial organizations have a role to play in this regard.[5]

The various chambers of commerce should bring stakeholders willing to buy and sell to each other. There is currently no India-Pakistan trade agreement, and Pakistan allows only a handful of commodities to be imported from India, which have, however, increased over the years. Nevertheless, despite the 615 items permissible for trade, 90 per cent of the trade takes place in only 42 items.[6]

However, as reported by the Indian PHD Chamber of Commerce in New Delhi, free interaction of the business community is curtailed as individual business visas for Indian group delegations are difficult to acquire. Group visas are the preferred means organized by the various chambers of commerce for exploring the market in Pakistan. These visas are often denied. When group visas are refused contacts made by Pakistani visiting delegations in India are eventually lost.

Opening up trade between Pakistan and India on an MFN basis would benefit Pakistani and Indian consumers. It would bring some of the smuggled goods into legal channels, especially if combined with a reduction in tariffs, bringing both governments badly needed customs revenues. It would also reduce the need for transit through third countries, reducing the transportation cost to consumers in both countries of goods that are being imported despite restrictions.

The importance of trade between India and Pakistan lies elsewhere. Businesses that are able to export successfully can be the

[5] Ibid.

[6] Government of Pakistan, Ministry of Commerce, *Pakistan-India Trade: Transition to the GATT Regime*, Islamabad, September 1996.

nucleus of badly needed peace constituencies. Interviews with an Indian Ministry of Commerce official suggest that in the past two to three years the trade environment has picked up. The third round of South Asian Preferential Trade Agreement (SAPTA) in 1999 was significant in this regard. The two countries exchanged concessions and eighteen tariff lines were reciprocated. Between 1999 and 2003, under the fourth round of SAARC, the two countries agreed to move beyond tokenism on the trade front and approximately 480 lines were given tariff exchanges. This allowed the signing of SAFTA on 6 January 2004. SAFTA will take effect from 1 January 2006 and the details of the framework are currently being negotiated.

There is hope in SAFTA. Sensitive lists are being reviewed by both countries. One suggestion is that instead of the list of 600-odd items that Pakistan allows for import from India it should draw a negative list of items that India should not be allowed to export to Pakistan to accommodate the fears of threatened industries in Pakistan. From Pakistan's point of view, tariffs and NTBs (non-tariff barriers) are a major hindrance in exporting to India. The NTBs, although they are not Pakistan specific need to be negotiated.

One of the most severe constraints is the lack of a free flow of information across the border. While most Indian commercial information is on the net, channels of communication need to be sustained in order to make room for negotiations. Trade talks between Indian and Pakistani commerce officials are underway, but so far no bilateral agreement has been reached.

From a trade perspective, a free-trade arrangement is a win-win situation for all concerned. However, due to political hitches, sustaining the process is the challenge. The risk element is high. Pakistan feels more comfortable in dealing with India through a regional framework rather than a bilateral agreement. When SAFTA takes shape there would be a sea change in the business environment. Indian tariffs would be decreased from 0 to 5 per cent, goods would be allowed to move more freely and industries would be set up across the border.

The Karachi Chambers of Commerce is also in favour of granting MFN status to India as it deems it in Pakistan's economic interest.

A study by the Karachi Chamber and Commerce and Industry also endorses the idea of trade with India, on the grounds that now having signed the agreements which have led to the setting up of the World Trade Organization, all signatory members have to be treated equally, and understands that giving Most Favored Nation status to India 'is not a special favor to India, but an obligation under WTO and an economic and geopolitical imperative.' In this new world order, the study argues, Pakistan has to face competition from all countries including India, and hence 'instead of shying away, we should be well prepared to face the eventuality. In any case, salvation lies in streamlining of operations and upgrading of technology which was long overdue.'[7]

India's imports are approximately 65–70 billion dollars annually. If Pakistan could compete for even 1 per cent of that figure it would contribute significantly to the GDP. Sixty per cent of Indian citizens depend on agriculture as a means of income generation, so the government tends to protect this sector with high tariffs. The peak tariff rate as of April 2004 was 20 per cent with the exception of automobiles and liqueur.[8] The ICRIER (Indian Council for Research on International Economic Relations) has proposed to the Indian government that it reduce its tariffs by 5 per cent to boost exports and strengthen productivity. Trade liberalization has been strongly recommended by the organization for a positive impact on Indian manufacturing.

Indian investors know that there are other foreign companies in Pakistan, however, the business community has to reach a greater level of comfort. Joint ventures may be one way of restoring the confidence and allaying the fears of the Pakistani industrialists. India and Pakistan need to develop business relationships to influence perceptions and attitudes.

The software industry in India is looking to analyse market

[7] Government of Pakistan, Ministry of Commerce, *Pakistan-India Trade: Transition to the GATT Regime*, Islamabad, September 1996.

[8] Interview with Arvind Virmani, ICRIER, New Delhi, 21 July 2004.

trends in Pakistan but free movement is constrained. Collaborative initiatives with the Indian software industry could help Pakistan compete in the international market.

All said and done, to quote the Indian Minister for Petroleum, Manisha Karaya, the country's trade regime needs to be more generous and willing to accommodate Pakistani fears. In an interview for this study, C. Raja Mohan has suggested that India should consider unilaterally opening up its trade with Pakistan.

India is now ranked as the third-largest investor in Sri Lanka after Japan and the USA. It also has an FTA with Nepal. The FTA encouraged a few north Indian companies to set up in Nepal where the production of consumer goods, such as toothpaste was cheaper. In the last couple of years Nepal has become the biggest exporter of tooth paste to India, and at the same time, India has become the biggest exporter to Nepal. This suggests that perhaps economic interdependence is no longer avoidable.[9]

Indian businessmen dealing in textile machinery are selling goods to Pakistan through third countries. Indian textile machinery is cheaper than the German and Swiss product by 50 per cent and delivery is faster. In addition, the machinery is more suited to Pakistani requirements. Automobile components are also finding their way across informally as Japanese car components are considerably more expensive. Tyres and tea are also being shipped through Dubai and elsewhere. Although these two are on the list of permissible items the supply chain through the third country has not been broken and the direct supply route not taken due to political instability. Fears that communication links may be disrupted again is clearly an apprehension in the minds of entrepreneurs.[10]

As this example suggests, with improved regional trade ties, India's neighbours would have greater access to the large Indian market, but the flow of trade would probably remain in India's favour. India now exports a wide range of commodities to Bangladesh, Nepal, Bhutan, and Sri Lanka, but its imports from these

[9] Interview with Nagesh Kumar.
[10] Ibid.

countries are limited. India is the leading source of imported goods for both Bangladesh and Sri Lanka and both run significant trade deficits with India. In order to allay apprehensions that trade liberalization would marginalize smaller countries in the region, key players would need to find ways of expanding exports from the smaller SAARC trading partners.

Conversations with stakeholders in India and Pakistan suggest that they are convinced of the benefits of greater economic cooperation. Many businessmen also have emotional ties across the border and have a special interest in trade.

Increased trade would also build both countries' capacity to compete in the international market. Both have been trying to open their economies amidst fears of undermining the local industries. Trading with the 'enemy' would also send the right kind of message to international investors as far as political and regional stability is concerned.

To make the most out of trade liberalization, however, it is important to work out an India-Pakistan trade agreement that provides tangible short-term benefits to both sides. A crucial element in providing these benefits is an economic policy that favours export-led growth.

CHAPTER 6

Recommendations

The success of the Indo-Pakistan peace process is important from an economic point of view. It may pave the way towards free movement and free trade. Presently, the boundaries are blocked with all kinds of barriers to free trade, from restrictions on travel to the free flow of goods, tariffs, non-tariff barriers, and quotas, to name a few of the stumbling blocks.

Interviews with stakeholders in both countries suggest that facilitating travel across the border would allow traders to discover goods and a demand for goods would be created. Markets should be allowed to decide what is tradable. Therefore, free movement and free interaction of the business communities would be the first logical step to economic cooperation.[1] In addition, telecom, travel and transport facilities for businessmen need to be maximized. India and Pakistan need to consider giving entrepreneurs multiple-entry visas that are valid for years. At the same time, arbitration arrangements entailing foolproof legislative mechanisms to allow free economic activity between the two countries need to be put in place.[2]

Unfortunately, however, since partition economic judgement has been clouded by political issues. If economic judgement were to prevail, then if a party is providing another with goods it wouldn't want to eliminate the buyer and, conversely, the other would not want to destroy its supply line. In fact, a shift towards interdependence and regional development would push the parties towards participation rather than antagonism. Free trade between two neighbours allows economic activity to be optimally productive and efficient.

[1] Interview with Sanjaya Baru, New Delhi, 17 July 2004.

[2] Interview with Arvind Virmani.

It is quite likely that once the doors of economic cooperation are opened it will not be feasible to close them again. When trade begins to flourish and both sides perceive the benefits of cooperation, communication links would be strengthened and secured. It may also be seen that economic CBMs can help build political differences where levels of mistrust are high.

An integrated regional economy helps to accelerate economic growth. Higher investment rates are the single factor giving South-East Asian economies an edge over South Asian economy. The minimum growth rate required for decreasing poverty is 7.5 per cent, which cannot be achieved without regional cooperation. The growth capacity of the regional economies needs to be restructured.[3] Regional economic integration is driven by industrial investment and industrial restructuring.

Speaking hypothetically of the automobile industry, for instance, if one country were to specialize in the production of tractors and the other in small cars, both countries could develop a comparative advantage as well as trade potential. The premise on which the European Union was created was not trade but a single market plan. In the EU, Ford now makes all its Escorts in the UK and Fiestas in Belgium. As a result, both plants are more efficient. The economies of scale are higher and the output better and sustainable.[4]

As mentioned earlier there is tremendous potential for economic cooperation between India and Pakistan due to factors such as geographical proximity, cultural and aesthetic similarities. Even in industries where the two states are apparently competing with each other there is potential for cooperation. Opening up trade and tourism would, therefore, help Pakistan and India release their economic potential. Through obsessive trading with India, Pakistan could add the 3 per cent to its rate of economic growth required to make a positive impact on the poverty pool.[5]

[3] Akmal Hussain, 'Peace, Poverty and Economic Growth in South Asia: A Policy Framwork', paper presented at the Institute of Regional Studies Conference in Islamabad, June 2004.

[4] Interview with Nagesh Kumar.

[5] Akmal Hussain, 'Peace, Poverty and Economic Growth', op. cit.

While the India-Pakistan balance of trade currently favours the former, Pakistani products have great market potential in India. As mentioned earlier, the 'Made in Pakistan' trade fair, a historic exhibition by Pakistani businessmen in New Delhi, held in March 2004, was an instant sell-out. It aimed to boost trade between India and Pakistan as well as allay concerns that a South Asian free-trade zone would lead to Indian goods flooding Pakistani markets. The trade fair, which was the first of its kind in India had close to three hundred exhibitors participating from across the border. Contracts worth millions of dollars were signed. Pakistan's leading entrepreneurs brought back good business.

Corporate sector profiles may also be developed to explore how many companies in India and Pakistan can work with each other.[6] Direct and formal trade would not only make it more feasible to trade but the governments also stand to generate more revenue if the third country route could be avoided. Third country trade is naturally highly costly. If India and Pakistan export to the West or elsewhere, they have to study the market, but trading with each other does not require such research. Language and distance are not barriers either. For instance, Latin America and Poland have now come up as great markets but distance, transportation costs, and language do not favour conditions conducive for trade.[7]

A CASE FOR FREE TRADE BETWEEN INDIA AND PAKISTAN

- Commonality of spoken language
- Short distance with lower freight
- Quick deliveries leading to short inventories
- Familiarity with each others' trade practices, fashions and needs
- Complementarity in several areas between the two countries

**Source*: PHD Chamber of Commerce and Industry, New Delhi.

[6] Interview with Poonam Barua, New Delhi, 22 July 2004.
[7] Interview with Shabnam Parekh, New Delhi, 23 July 2004.

POTENTIAL ITEMS OF EXPORT TO PAKISTAN FROM INDIA

- Electric cables
- Chemicals
- Cement
- Small hand tools
- Coconut oil
- Cashew nuts
- Coir yarn and products
- Long staple cotton
- Silk—dress material
- Coffee
- Tea
- Tyres and tubes
- Iron ore
- Organic and inorganic chemicals
- Dyes and dyestuffs
- Drugs and medicines
- Industrial and medical gases
- Railway track material
- Construction machinery
- Steel
- Engine industries
- Agricultural machinery—combine harvesters
- Office equipment—computers
- Drawing machines
- Pumps, boilers and parts
- Special steels
- Power-generating and distribution equipment
- Oil-prospecting equipment
- Chemical machinery
- Railway equipment
- Fishing equipment
- Nickel screens for the continuous centrifugal machine for sugar mills

- Pentaerythritol (for manufacturing alkyd resin for air-drying paints

Source: PHD Chamber of Commerce and Industry, New Delhi and interviews with stakeholders.

POTENTIAL ITEMS OF EXPORT TO INDIA FROM PAKISTAN

- Raw cotton of small and medium staples
- Raw wool
- Dairy products
- Flowers
- Fruits
- Spices
- Processed foods
- Sugar and molasses
- Scrap iron (required for electric furnaces)
- Carpets (knotted and machine made)
- Cotton fabrics
- Fresh and dried fruits and vegetables
- Dry fruit
- Fish (fresh and frozen)
- Scrap tyres and rubbers
- Rock salt
- Naphtha
- Gypsum
- Marble and onyx
- Industrial alcohol/alcoholic beverages
- Rock phosphate
- Granite rocks
- Sulphur chemicals
- Limestone
- Fertilizer
- Natural gas
- Electricity
- Herbs

- Unani medicinal preparations
- Artificial resins and plastic materials
- Soda ash
- Pearls and semi-precious stones
- Agro-chemicals
- Automotive components
- Surgical instruments
- Sports goods
- Canned juices
- Shuttle looms
- Dental operating systems
- Air conditioning/deep freezers
- Finished textile goods
- Finished leather and leather goods.

Source: PHD Chamber of Commerce and Industry, New Delhi, and interviews with stakeholders.

AREAS OF SCOPE FOR INVESTMENT COOPERATION

Energy

The most significant economic benefit of cooperation between India and Pakistan lies in energy cooperation.[8] India is one of the fastest growing energy markets in the world and will be looking for more sources of supply within the region. India and Pakistan together possess an abundance of water, forest, coal, and gas, which are the principal sources of energy. In addition high rainfall and mountainous terrain in the Himalayan regions provide tremendous potential for generating hydropower. Unfortunately, however, the poor quality of energy infrastructure, inequitable distribution of available energy, and inaccessible and

[8] Mahendar P. Lama, 'Economic Reforms and the Energy Sector in South Asia: Scope for Cross-Border Power Trade', in *South Asia Survey*, vol. 7, no. 1, New Delhi, 2000; Mahendar P. Lama, and Rasul Bakhsh Rais, 'Pipelines and Power Grids for Peace', International Centre for Peace Initiatives, Mumbai, 2001; and *India Pakistan Economic Relations: A Report*, FICCI, New Delhi, March 2004.

and costly energy availability has resulted in slow growth and development.

At present both countries are heavy energy importers and are confronted by a growing disparity between the demand for and the supply of power. Industrialization and increasing household requirements will continue to add to this demand. The private sector in both countries has been actively involved in the energy generation sector. Independent Power Producers (IPP) have been at the forefront of investments in this area. India and Pakistan can work together to share their experiences and explore means for generating the energy required to meet their needs.

Pakistan has the largest gas reserves in South Asia giving it an edge over India in the energy sector. Pakistan also produces about 3,000 Mega Watt (MW) of surplus power. India is a potential market for this energy. Pakistan could become a major supplier of energy to the noth-western states of India. However, Pakistan's potential role in fulfilling India's need will not be as a supplier but as a transit route for energy from other countires.

> Pakistan has the potential to increase the supply of both gas and hydelpower well beyond even the more optimistic projections of increase in domestic demand. Some 100 undeveloped dam sites have been identified by various groups of exports which could generate an additional 35,000 MW of electricity. The country also has coal reserves of 85 billion tons, the second largest deposits in South Asia. China, which produces a significant amount of electricity from coal and where coal still accounts for 80 per cent of electirc power generation, is helping Pakistan to develop coal-powered electric generation. Once developed, this would add to the surplus of power Pakistan will have available for sale.[9]

As menioned earlier, India and Pakistan, both of which will require large volumes of natural gas imports to meet their future

[9] Shahid Javed Burki, 'Pakistan, India and Regional Cooperation', in the *South Asian Journal*, April–June 2004.

domestic needs, can tap the major gas deposits of the Persian Gulf and Central Asia. Of the several options available, the import of natural gas through a pipeline from neighbouring countries like Qatar, Oman, Iran, Bangladesh and Turkmenistan is being explored and is the most cost-effective way. An overland joint natural gas pipeline from Pakistan to India would be more economically viable for both countries than constructing independent pipelines (see Tables 6.1 and 6.2).

TABLE 6.1: INDEPENDENT PIPELINE/LNG OPTION*

Pipeline	India	Pakistan
Turkmenistan	2.40	1.50
Iran (Onshore)	4.00 (LNG)	1.50
Gulf States	2.90 (LNG)	2.60 (LNG)

TABLE 6.2: JOINT PIPELINE*

India	Pakistan
1.80	1.20
1.80	1.20
2.50	2.00

Notes: * In US $ per MBTU of natural gas
LNG: Liquefied natural gas
BCMY: Billion cubic metres per year
MBTU: Million British thermal units
kWh: kiloWatt/hour

Source: *Cost of Conflict between India and Pakistan*, Strategic Foresight Group, Mumbai, 2004.

A project proposal submitted by Iran to both countries estimated that Pakistan could earn approximately US $600–800 million per pipeline per year in transit rights. It would also be able to use the pipelines to fulfil its domestic requirements. For India, on the other hand, importing gas through the pipeline would serve as a cheaper option than imports of the costly liquid natural gas (LNG). If there is a drop in LNG prices, India would still be at a significant cost advantage by getting its supply from Iran through Pakistan. In addition, mega projects of the nature of gas pipelines will also make a huge psychological difference towards creating an environment of trust and confidence.The Indian bureaucracy has shown some reservations regarding the oil pipeline from Central Asian States via Pakistan; however it needs to remember that the USSR supplied oil to Western Europe at the peak of the Cold War.

Entrepreneurs and industrial lobbies on both sides of the divide need to lobby with politicians for energy cooperation (as well as in other sectors) as the governments on both sides appear to be locked in their political positions. Business associations can also be used as a reliable face-saving mechanism by both governments.

Monetary incentives for Pakistani businesses would motivate them to influence the government. Awareness may also be raised through media campaigns. The pipeline may be financed jointly by India, Pakistan, and international financial institutions. The level of risk for India would be minimized if Pakistan had an equal stake in protecting the pipeline.

Pakistan, which has not exploited the solar energy technology on a large-scale due to high costs and institutional problems, can benefit from India, which has the world's largest solar energy programme.

Interlinked power and gas networks will generate interdependence between Pakistan and India, which may help to reduce costs in an effective manner and make power and natural gas imports economically viable.

Transit Route

Apart from trade, the SAARC countries are among the least economically integrated in the world. Pakistan's geographic location is ideally suited to make it the hub of regional and international trade. There are currently no regular transport links between India and Pakistan.

Even if this situation were restored to 'normal', regional transportation links are poor. As with trade, geography dictates that land transportation links are between India and each of its neighbors, but even air links among the six smaller SAARC countries are few and far between. Where the land borders are open, restrictive trucking laws result in enormous inefficiencies as goods are transferred by hand (or, more accurately, by head) from truck to truck. Common infrastructure is almost nonexistent. Both these factors further depress the already anemic regional trade.[10]

Apart from travel restrictions, the trade routes by train (Atari route) and the sea route by Mumbai are not adequate. The PHD (Punjab, Haryana, New Delhi) Chamber of Commerce suggests opening up of more border points and a road route for trade.

If India could use Pakistan as a transit route for trade with Central Asian and Persian Gulf states, it would boost its level of trade relations tremendously. It would also be highly beneficial for border states and towns to trade with each other, particularly the two Punjabs, Haryana, Rajasthan and Sindh. Pakistan is the natural gateway for landlocked Afghanistan's trade through the port city of Karachi. Pakistan will need to enhance the communications infrastructure, such as roads, railways, ports, and airports.[11]

In order to provide transit services, it will need to provide services such as warehousing, refrigeration, processing, insurance, and trans-shipment. Communications infrastructure, road, rail and air links need to be enhanced and upgraded to facilitate cross-border trade. Where there is commonality of skills, such as in the production of designer wear India and Pakistan can also venture jointly into West Asia, Central Asia and Iran. Pakistan already has contacts and trading partners in these countries.

Textiles and Textile Machinery

Both India and Pakistan are cotton-growing countries. They have a well-established cotton industry and are a source of raw cotton and cotton products for the global market. Pakistan has a competitive advantage in cotton textile products while India is competitive in silk and other synthetic fibre products. The opening up of trade will enable Pakistan to acquire textile chemicals and

[10] Schaffer, 'Regional Economic Relationships', op. cit.

[11] Interview with C. Raja Mohan, New Delhi, 23 July 2004.

other inputs at cheaper rates and thus make its products more competitive in the international market. Finished Pakistani textile goods such as bed linen, which has swamped the EU market, will also find buyers in India. In addition Pakistani fabric for *shalwar qameez* the traditional dress worn in Pakistan is very popular in India. Free movement of textile entrepreneurs will allow Pakistan to boost its textile exports. It would help the goods to sell in larger volumes in geographically proximate markets besides impacting positively on agricultural and industrial growth. The interaction with the Indian market will also give the Pakistanis free access to other markets in the South Asian region as India has Free Trade Agreements with most of them. Pakistani textiles will, therefore, inevitably find their way across to Sri Lanka and Nepal, amongst others.

On the other hand, Pakistan does not possess a high-tech textile machinery industry. Opening up trade with India would help it to acquire this technology at a much lower price and in much less time if they were to import the high-cost machinery from Germany and Switzerland. This item is presently not permissible for import from India.[12]

Therefore, it is clear that despite the Indian and Pakistani edge in the international cotton market complementarity of interests does exist and both countries can cut costs and generate more revenue by relying on each other's strengths.

Tourism

Tourism is rated as the largest industry in the world. It contributes over 12 per cent to the world GDP and has created employment for over 210 million people (accounting for over 10.7 per cent of the global workforce)[13] directly or indirectly. There are tremendous opportunities for the promotion of tourism between India and Pakistan. So far it has been severely limited due to travel restrictions and the unsuitable political environment.

India's tourism sector provides direct employment to over

[12] Interview with Nagesh Kumar.

[13] SAARC reports.

8.5 million (2.4 people of the total labour force). Over 100 million domestic tourists visit different parts of the country every year. The Indian model could be replicated by Pakistan to develop the infrastructural requirements and an Indo-Pak joint tourism visa (along the lines of the Schengen visa) may be offered to tourists. The amazing tourist attractions in Pakistan such as the fabled Indus Civilization, the Buddha Gandhara period, the heritage of the Mughal period and the British Raj are of immense interest to outsiders.

As interviews with Pakistani and Indian stakeholders show, there is call for Pakistan and India to facilitate tourism across the borders. Citizens of both countries are constrained from travelling next door although there is a huge demand for visit to holy sites on both sides of the border. In addition, both countries offer attractive destinations for cultural, historical, and adventure tourism. Business, medical, heritage, and religious tourism are areas in which travel restrictions should be relaxed. This will enhance people-to-people contact and encourage sociocultural interaction. Simplified visa regulations may be considered to encourage the flow of tourism.

The Pakistani tourism authorities would do well to learn the marketing strategies of their neighbour. Pakistan has to its advantage the world's second highest peak, Karakoram 2, decidedly more breathtaking than Mount Everest. Fascinating cities like Lahore, Peshawar, and Karachi are a delight for visitors. The kite-flying season of *Basant* and similar cultural festivals attract tourists from around the world. Boosting the tourism industry will make a positive impact on the growth of a business environment and investment opportunities. More jobs will be created and poverty will be alleviated.

Goa in India and other similar destinations would attract a lot of tourists from Pakistan who otherwise spend money travelling to nearby locations such as the Far East.

Agriculture

India and Pakistan are both agricultural economies and there is immense scope for collaboration in this sector. Agriculture provides jobs and generates the income of over half the population in both countries. Liberalized trade in the food and agri-business would generate hundreds of thousands of jobs in both countries. Pakistani and Indian cottons are of different varieties and could be bartered.

Pakistani raw cotton is in great demand in India. Pakistan could provide raw cotton for the needs of the entire north Indian belt. Additionally India may also consider buying all the raw cotton being produced by Pakistan as by the end 2005, the former is likely to face a severe shortage of raw cotton.[14]

India has been exporting palm to Pakistan and could look into planting palm farms there. It could also offer mushroom production technology to Pakistan.

Indian horticultural expertise in the production of flowers can also be capitalized upon. Floriculture plants may be set up in Pakistan to jointly produce and export flowers to the rest of the world. Pakistan may also develop its own expertise in this area and provide flowers to India to meet its needs.[15]

Joint ventures could be set up for the production of agricultural crops and also for processing of produce. The processed products may be traded officially and third country markets could also be jointly explored.

Both countries have the potential for developing the food-processing industry. Although India is one of the top producers of milk, fish, fruits and vegetables in the world hardly 1 per cent of its horticultural production is processed. The constraints faced by the food processing industry in both countries are poor, inadequate infrastructure, poor quality of raw materials including non-availability in bulk, low productivity of various horticultural crops, poor quality of packaging, insufficient working capital, and lack of grading facilities and standards. Given the commonality of an agrarian-based economy, both countries could collaborate in developing the food processing industry.[16]

Increased trade in agricultural commodities, vegetables, and fruits may be one of the first steps to be considered seriously.

[14] Interview with S. Narayan, New Delhi, 21 July 2004.

[15] 'PHDCCI Delegation to Pakistan—A Report', 28 July–2 August 1997, New Delhi.

[16] Ibid.

Subsequently, the exchange of processed foods with longer shelf life could be negotiated.

Tea

South Asia has about 28 per cent of its area under total world tea production and produces approximately 42 per cent of the total tea produced globally. Tea has a very vast market in South Asia itself. It is estimated that the region alone consumes over 900 million kg of tea annually.[17]

Pakistan a major importer of tea in the world, has been importing an overwhelming proportion of its domestic requirements from countries outside the region. Its formal tea imports have steadily grown from 51 million kg in 1975 to 124 million kg in 1994, thus taking it into the category of the top three importers, with an 11 per cent share in total world tea imports (see Table 6.3). It is estimated that Pakistan actually brings in 150 million kg of tea, of which 40 million kg is smuggled, thereby making it the largest importer of tea in the world (14.71 per cent of total world imports of 1,019.42 million kg). It is Kenya that has emerged as the most vital source of Pakistan's tea imports, bagging over 60 per cent in 1995 as against a meager 11 per cent in 1975. Ironi-

TABLE 6.3: PAKISTAN'S COST OF TEA IMPORTS

Source	Quantity (million kg)			Unit values ($/kg)		
	1992	1993	1994	1992	1993	1994
SAARC region	21.15	17.68	20.83	1.59	1.43	1.48
Outside the region	99.14	95.91	103.29	2.14	1.80	1.67
Cost of non-cooperation ($ million)				54.52	35.48	19.62

Source: Mahender P. Lama, 'Integrating the Tea Sector in South Asia: New Opportunities in the Global Market', in *South Asian Survey*, vol. 8, no. 1, 2001.

[17] For a more detailed discussion see Mahendar P. Lama, 'Integrating the Tea Sector in South Asia: New Opportunities in the Global Market', in *South Asian Survey*, vol. 8, no. 1, 2001, New Delhi.

cally, South Asia has been both the largest and geographically the nearest possible tea producer for Pakistan to access. India has never been a major source of tea imports for Pakistan.[18]

Records for the past three decades indicate that Pakistan has never imported more than 1.5 per cent of its total imports from India. It has been importing tea from outside the region at a much higher price than it would have from within South Asia. Estimates for the year 1992–94 reveal the increasing cost of non-cooperation and benefits that could have accrued out of cooperation. Indian and Pakistani tea conglomerates need to chalk out a strategy to take advantage of the newly emerging markets. There is high scope for investment potentialities in Pakistan. A clear strategy that largely encompasses replantation, filling in vacancies where the density of tea cultivation is low, consistent and continuous replanting of old seedling tea with vegetative propagated tea, increasing the adoption of proper cultural practices such as fertilization, weeding and adherence to the correct pruning style needs to be thought out.[19]

Drugs and Pharmaceuticals

Bulk drugs produced in Pakistan are more expensive than those produced in India. For example, Fosamax is almost eighteen times more expensive in Pakistan then in India; ciprofloxacin is about five times costlier; and diclofenic is approximately ten times more expensive. General health conditions and life expectancy in both India and Pakistan remain poor and low.

The market for the pharmaceutical sector in Pakistan and India has been maintaining a growth of 15 per cent. The per capita consumption of drugs and pharmaceuticals in Pakistan was about US $8.5 during 1996–7 compared to US $3.4 in India. Hence, new investments in the pharmaceutical sector in the former can readily replace imported drugs in the market. The Indian pharma industry is one of the largest and most advanced amongst developing countries. It produces a wide range of basic drugs and

[18] Ibid.

[19] Ibid.

pharmaceuticals, including various therapeutic regimes such as antibiotics, hormones, steroids, vaccines, herbal preparation, etc. It is capable of meeting about 90 per cent of the country's requirements of bulk drugs and almost the entire demand for formulations. Owing to its strength in technology for bulk drugs, India has become a net exporter in the pharmaceutical sector.[20]

Indian companies and research institutes such as the National Institute of Pharmaceutical Education and Research, which has been declared a centre of excellence, can assist in the development of the pharma sector in Pakistan.[21] The joint venture arrangements can be in terms of supply of technology, R&D assistance, and marketing support.

Research and Development

Industry has a tendency to shift to where production is cheaper and regional hubs can be created, specializing in different areas. India and Pakistan could collaborate in the areas of bio-technology, environment and water management, poverty alleviation, economic liberalization, inter alia. There is currently no forum for sharing of information and best practices. India's knowledge-based industry has tremendous potential.[22] It is the preferred destination for research and development as compared to China. It possesses highly trained manpower in the areas of science and technology. Many countries across the globe find India to be a competitive market for outsourcing. It has attained a competitive edge in the software industry, pharmaceuticals, and the auto industry.

Engineering and Light Engineering

Trade liberalization with India, especially for iron ore which is an important raw material for steel industries, will place the engi-

[20] *Status Paper: India Pakistan Economic Relations*, FICCI, New Delhi, 2003; and 'A Study on Prospects for India-Pakistan Economic Partnership', FICCI, New Delhi, 2001.

[21] SAARC data.

[22] Interview with R.K. Pachauri, TERI, New Delhi, 20 July 2004.

neering goods industry of Pakistan at a significant advantage by bringing down prices of steel by 50 per cent and that of finished engineering goods by 10 to 20 per cent. Pakistan is currently importing iron ore at a very high cost from Brazil and Argentina.

Technology may also be sourced from India to set up an LPG cylinder manufacturing unit in Pakistan. There is also scope for the inclusion of cylinders for natural gases.[23]

Information Technology

India is a global IT super power and has taken a lead in the information revolution. The software industry in India has been one of the fastest growing industries in terms of both exports and domestic use. For India, software exports have been the greatest foreign exchange earners since 1991.[24] In the area of customized software services, India commands a significant market share in the world ranking fifth in exports after US, Japan, Ireland and Germany.[25] While in Pakistan the telecommunications sector is developing very fast creating a very high interest in FDI.

Both countries could makes immense strides in economic growth by working together to bring the region in the forefront of the IT world. The technology is called for by the trends in globalization and would aid telecommunication development, growth of all business sectors and increasing FDI inflows. India could be the role model and both countires could collaborate to tap the large global market for software[26] by establishing software exports training centers and software development centers. An increasing number of foreign companies rely on Indian expertiese for outsourcing their IT requirements at relatively competitive rates. By sharing of best practices and specialized training of the growing Pakistani IT labour force unlimited opportunities for employment would be generated.

[23] *Status Paper: India Pakistan Economic Relations*, FICCI, New Delhi, 2003; and 'India-Pakistan Economic Relations: A Report, FICCI, New Delhi, 2004.

[24] *Status Paper: India Pakistan Economic Relations*, FICCI, New Delhi, March 2003.

[25] SAARC reports.

[26] *Status Paper: India Pakistan Economic Relations*, FICCI, New Delhi, March 2003.

Fish Processing

Fisheries are an important economic activity providing direct and indirect employment to millions of people. India and Pakistan have tremendous potential for the development of this industry through production and international marketing. India is one of the top producers of fish and Pakistan also possesses large fish stocks, but most of these have not been commercially exploited. Processing of frozen and canned fish products as well as production of canned exports to developed countries needs to be explored for mutual advantage. Development of this sector would also stimulate the ship industry.[27]

Agro-chemicals

With the expansion of agri-business there is a growing demand for agro-chemicals. Indian technology may be transferred to Pakistan. Pesticides manufacturing units could be set up in Pakistan. This would go a long way in supporting the agricultural economy of the country.[28]

Chemicals

Indian players and multinationals can asist Pakistan in developing this sector by setting up dyes and pigments manufacturing unit in Pakistan.[29]

Automobile Ancillary

This industry has grown rapidly over the years in India and Pakistan. India takes a lead in the manufacture of passenger cars in the SAARC region. Next to India, Pakistan is the only country in the region to manufacture and assemble passenger cars. Pakistan and India could work on an integrated auto component complex.[30]

[27] SAARC reports.

[28] *Status Paper: India Pakistan Economic Relations*, FICCI, New Delhi, March 2003.

[29] Ibid.

[30] Ibid.

Pakistan may also consider assembly of heavy and light vehicles in collaboration with India. While India has managed the indigenization process in the auto industry successfully to the benefit of its local consumers, Pakistan needs to develop the automotive sector to meet future demand.

Leather Processing Complex: Value Added Products for Exports

Pakistan has a strong manufacturing base for leather. It manufactures a variety of value added leather footwear, garments and bags. By sharing the skill in craftsmanship Pakistan and India could cooperate to tap the global market and expand their global market share.[31]

[31] Ibid.

CHAPTER 7

Concluding Remarks

Enhanced bilateral cooperation is an imperative if Pakistan and India are to strengthen their economies, both individually and as regional partners, so as to attract foreign capital from outside and even within the region to widen and diversify their production base. Economic cooperation would protect their individual economies in the face of the rapid pace of globalization, to maximize the benefits and minimize the costs of the process.

The two countries India and Pakistan have certain inherent advantages in bilateral cooperation. They have the advantage of geographical contiguity and shared economic, social, and cultural characteristics, which should serve to reduce the transaction costs. They also share an inherited development infrastructure.

Trade liberalization would not only enhance economic productivity and efficiency, it would also have a positive impact on social welfare and poverty alleviation. The consumers and the government, two major stakeholders, would benefit from lower prices and greater customs revenue from legalizing illicit border trade, respectively. Improved transportation links, communications, research and development, regional trade financing, customs cooperation, and relaxing travel restrictions for traders would enhance the regional development infrastructure. Greater economic activity would also help reduce poverty by increasing employment, income generation, trade augmentation, and development at large.

A sustained multi-tier economic partnership between India and Pakistan will also help build trust and confidence between the two countries. A relationship that is mutually beneficial should motivate the adversaries to move towards the resolution of political differences and become partners in development. A composite dialogue to address bilateral political disputes is already underway. Trade may prove to have much larger gains then socio-economic development alone. Opening up channels of communication and avenues for cooperation may be the first step towards the stabilization of relations in a nuclear environment.

APPENDIX 1

INTERVIEWS CONDUCTED IN NEW DELHI

1. Sanjaya Baru, Media Adviser to Prime Minister Manmohan Singh
2. Ashok K. Lahiri, Chief Economic Adviser, Ministry of Finance and Company Affairs
3. C. Raja Mohan, Professor of South Asian Studies, Jawaharlal Nehru University
4. S.S. Kapur, Joint Secretary, Ministry of Commerce and Industry
5. R.K. Pachauri, Director General, The Energy and Resources Institute
6. Gen. (retired) A.N. Vohra
7. Bharat Karnad, Research Professor, Centre for Policy Research
8. Nagesh Kumar, Director General, Research and Information System for the Non-Aligned and other Developing countries (RIS)
9. Mahendra P. Lama, Professor of South Asian Economies and Chief Economic Adviser to the Chief Minister of Sikkim
10. Arvind Virmani, Director and Chief Executive, Indian Council for Research on International Economic Relations (ICRIER)
11. Manish Mohan, Assistant Director, Federation of Indian Chambers of Commerce and Industry (FICCI)
12. Shabnam Parekh, Secretary (International Affairs), PHD Chamber of Commerce
13. S. Narayan, Former Economic Adviser to the Government of India
14. Poonam Barua, Regional Director–India, The Conference Board, New York
15. Charan Wadhwa, President and Chief Executive, Centre for Policy Research

16. Nisha Taneja, Research Fellow, Indian Council for Research on International Economic Relations (ICRIER)
17. Gen. Dipankar Banerji, Director General, Institute for Peace and Conflict Studies
18. R.S. Ahlawat, Additional Economic Adviser, Department of Economic Affairs
19. Yogesh Chandra, Adviser Department of Economic Affairs

INTERVIEWS CONDUCTED IN ISLAMABAD

1. Shahid Bashir, Joint Secretary & Director General Ministry of Commerce
2. Ashfaque H. Khan, Chief Economic Adviser, Ministry of Finance
3. Mariana Babar, Journalist
4. Tariq Zamir, Director India, Ministry of Foreign Affairs
5. Waqar Ahmed, Coordinator, SAARC Chamber of Commerce and Industry
6. Ayesha Siddiqa, Security Analyst
7. Brig. Tughral Yamin
8. Salma Malik, Lecturer, Department of Defence and Strategic Studies, Quaid-e-Azam University
9. Ayesha Moeen, Private Mutual Fund Manager, Islamabad Stock Exchange
10. Faisal Yousuf, Development Worker, CARITAS
11. Ahmed Ayub, Software Engineer, LMK Resources (Halliburton)
12. Imran Awan, Director, Minawa Private Limited (Construction firm)
13. Mushaf Zia, Former Pakistani Tennis Champion and Davis Cup Player
14. Imran Aman, Chief Executive, Kashan Carpets
15. Moeen Manzoor, Assistant Vice-President, First Dawood Investment Bank
16. Mehrunisa Jehangir, Legal Officer, Marri Gas

RCSS PUBLICATIONS

- *Defence, Technology and Cooperative Security in South Asia: Report on the Proceedings of the Tenth Summer Workshop* (RCSS, 2004)
- *Environment Development and Human Security: Perspectives from South Asia* (2003)
- *Terrorism in South Asia: Impact on Development and Democratic Process* (SIPRA, 2003)
- *South Asia and the War on Terrorism* (India Research Press, 2003)
- *Shaping the Future–A South Asian Civil Society Dialogue* (RCSS, July 2002)
- *Small Arms and Human Insecurity* (RCSS, July 2002)
- *SAARC in the Twenty-First Century: Towards a Cooperative Future* (July 2002)
- *Memories of a Genocidal Partition: The Haunting Tale of Victims, Witnesses and Perpetrators* (RCSS, July 2002)
- *South Asian Security Futures: A Dialogue of Director's Regional Strategic Studies Institutes* (March 2002)
- *Security and Governance in South Asia* (September 2001)
- *Globalization and Non-Traditional Security in South Asia* (September 2001)
- *Security in the New Millennium* (India Research Press, 2001)
- *The Simla Agreement 1972-Its Wasted Promise* (Manohar, 2001)

RCSS Newsletter

A quarterly bulletin, it publishes a brief report of RCSS activities, presentations at its workshops on topics of contemporary interest and news and programmes of the RCSS and its alumnae.

RCSS Policy Studies

35 Nuclear Risk Reduction Measures in South Asia: Problems and Prospects (Manohar, forthcoming)
34 Indo-Pak Conflicts: Ripe to Resolve? (Manohar, 2005)
33 Small Arms and the Security Debate in South Asia (Manohar, 2005)
32 New Nuclear Triangle and China's Role in South Asia (forthcoming)
31 Stability through Economic Cooperation in a Nuclear Environment (Manohar, 2005)
30 Multi-Track Diplomacy between India and Pakistan: A Conceptual Framework for Sustainable Security (Manohar, 2005)
29 The Role of Mediation in Resolving India-Pakistan Conflict: Parameters and Possibilities (Manohar, 2005)
28 HIV/AIDS as a Security Threat to India (Manohar, 2005)
27 Nepal's Maoist Movement and Implications for India and China (Manohar, 2005)
26 Elite Perceptions in Foreign Policy: Role of Print Media in Influencing India-Pakistan Relations, 1989–1999 (Manohar, 2004)
25 Nuclar Risk Reduction Measures and Restraint Regime in South Asia (Manohar, 2004)
24 River Water Sharing Problem Between India and Pakistan: Case Study of the Indus Basin Water Treaty (June 2004)
23 Christianity and Political Conflict in India: The Case of Gujarat (June 2002)

Fellowship in South Asian Alternatives (FISAA) Monograph

- Water, Power And People: A South Asian Manifesto on the Politics and Knowledge of Water (1997)
- The Nuclear Debate: Ironies and Immoralities (1998)

Others

- *Directory of Individuals and Institutions Engaged in South Asian Strategic Studies* (1998).